PRAISE FOR *HEART SI[STERS]*

"*Heart Sisters* is a beautiful reminder of how powerful walking hand in hand with a loyal friend can be. After reading this book, your heart will long to be this kind of God-honoring friend. Thank you, Natalie, for the charge to sacrificially love and serve our friends."

—**Lysa TerKeurst**, *New York Times* best-selling author of *The Best Yes* and president of Proverbs 31 Ministries

"In today's highly connected world, we can find ourselves leading surprisingly lonely lives because what we long for is not one more 'friend' on social media but relationships where we're truly known. Here's the good news: It doesn't have to stay that way. Natalie Snapp helps us find (and be) the kind of heart sister we've been searching for all along."

—**Holley Gerth**, *Wall Street Journal* best-selling author of *You're Already Amazing*

"We need our girlfriends, but sometimes those relationships are challenging to navigate! This is a how-to guide on women's friendships that every woman needs."

—**Jill Savage**, CEO of Hearts at Home and author of *No More Perfect Moms*

"Friends. We all want them yet struggle to find and keep them! In *Heart Sisters*, Natalie Snapp empowers women to find and be the type of friend that we are not only looking for but truly want to be. A great tool for helping us find the missing link between the relationships we have and the relationships we desire."

—**Lynn Cowell**, speaker with Proverbs 31 Ministries and author of *Magnetic: Becoming the Girl He Wants*

"As someone who grew up in a home with three younger sisters, a Mom, and a girl dog and who ended up in full-time women's ministry, I am passionately aware that relationships with other women can be tough sometimes! Natalie Chambers Snapp writes with refreshing honesty about the struggles she's encountered in her own relationships, how to establish boundaries that are healthy and holy, and how to teach our young girls to honor and respect one another. At a time when life is so busy that friendships often get pushed to the side, *Heart Sisters* is a much-needed reminder of the importance of other women in our lives."

—**Pat Layton**, author of *A Surrendered Life* and *Life Unstuck*

HEART SISTERS

Becoming the Friend You Want to Have

NATALIE CHAMBERS SNAPP

ABINGDON PRESS | NASHVILLE

HEART SISTERS
BECOMING THE FRIEND YOU WANT TO HAVE

Copyright © 2015 by Natalie Snapp

Library of Congress Cataloging-in-Publication Data

Snapp, Natalie Chambers.
  Heart sisters : becoming the friend you want to have / Natalie Chambers Snapp. — First
Edition.
    pages cm
  ISBN 978-1-4267-6905-4 (binding: soft back : alk. paper) 1. Christian women—Religious
life. 2. Female friendship—Religious aspects—Christianity. I. Title.
  BV4527.S63375 2015
  248.8'43—dc23

2014042897

The heart illustration on page 43 is by Eric Smoldt. www.ericsmoldt.com. Used by permission.

15 16 17 18 19 20 21 22 23 24—10 9 8 7 6 5 4 3 2 1
MANUFACTURED IN THE UNITED STATES OF AMERICA

To Jason, my true north
Who always finds a way.
Who is my biggest cheerleader.
Who walks through life with me, even when it's hard.

To Sarah
Improving the culture of women starts with your generation.
I'm so thankful and proud to be your mother.

To Samuel and Spencer
Believe it or not, Heart Sisters can influence boys, too.
A supportive and loving community of women will bless your
future wives more than you know.

To my mom, Sarah Lenox Quick, for modeling the importance
of friendship.

And of course, to my Heart Sisters
Jennifer, Katherine, Rachel J., Jen, Katrina,
Rachel S., Laurie, Shelly, Melinda, Jill, Kelli, and Dana
You know the ugly parts of my soul and love me anyway.
Thank you.

CONTENTS

A LETTER TO READERS

Hello, Sister.

I can already tell we'll be friends. By picking up this book, you tell me so much about who you are and what you believe.

You care about your relationships with other women. You wonder how to have deeper, more authentic female friendships. And you are more interested in encouraging and supporting other women than you are comparing and competing with other women.

Maybe you've also been wounded by a female friend in the past and your heart is filled with trepidation over the thought of opening it up to new friends. Maybe you're struggling to forgive a friend who has hurt you. Or maybe you wonder if you need to have a difficult conversation with a friend, and if so, what should you say?

Relationships aren't easy, friend. I really wish they were, but they're not. Anytime we invest our hearts, there's a chance they will get hurt. However, hurts from our relationships with women can especially sting. Unfortunately, I know this from experience. Fortunately, I've lived through it and was able to eventually seek and foster healthier female friendships as a result.

I know you can, too.

Sometimes, when we look back in our own lives, we start to see things more clearly. Now that I'm forty-one years old and a follower of Jesus, many of my tangled experiences are much more clear. I'm guessing I'm not alone in this, either. You could probably say the same about your own life, right?

The father role in my life has been a rotating door. I was born through artificial insemination because my father was sterile. In other words, I don't know the identity of my biological father.

I grew up in a small Midwestern town, the daughter of a wonderful mother and, sadly, a severely alcoholic father. My dad surfaced now and then when he was on the wagon; however, he disappeared when he was off the wagon. When I was six years old, my father's alcoholism ended my parents' marriage. My mother did everything she could to provide a normal, healthy childhood for me, and eventually she remarried. A new man stepped into the father's role.

In addition, I was bullied horribly in middle school and high school and experienced "mean girl" behavior in college. Admittedly, sometimes I was a *victim* of mean girls and sometimes I *was* the mean girl. I wish this weren't true, but I have to be real with you—I was.

A few years after college graduation, I married my college sweetheart. We settled into newlywed life and things were good—or so I thought. Six months after our wedding, our marriage started to crumble. We sought help and began to heal, but then a year later, old problems resurfaced and showed no signs of stopping.

To say I was devastated is putting in mildly. It didn't help that during the time when I moved out of the home we shared, my father's health began to fail. He died two months after I filed for divorce.

A more detailed account of my story can be found on my blog, but these two events, in combination with my other life experiences, brought me to my knees—literally.

I decided to train for a half marathon, which is hilarious because I had never run even a mile prior to this decision. Right before one of those runs, I grabbed the Michael W. Smith CD my aunt had given me and popped it in my Discman. (Can you believe we used to run with CD players on our arms?) I will never forget that run, that vehicle God placed on my heart because He knew it was the only way I would be alone with my thoughts. As I listened to so many beautiful songs about Jesus, I began to wonder.

I started to meet with a very patient and loving woman from an organization called Priority Associates. She answered my hard questions and presented the gospel to me for the first time. Turns out, what I thought was the end of my rope was actually just the beautiful beginning.

Two years later, I met a man who had also traveled a broken road. We fell in love, got married, had three children within four years, and moved to a new community. We've had our share of struggles, but through it all, our love for Jesus sustains us and motivates us to keep showing up each day.

During those sometimes lonely days of my childhood, I always wanted to have a real-life sister. We would play with dolls, love pink, wear sparkles in our hair, and tell late-night secrets. I know, Gender Stereotype Central.

But God didn't plan that for me.

He did, however, plan for me to have sisters of the heart.

Heart Sisters who didn't grow up with me but will stand up with me no matter what. Heart Sisters who know my most horrible qualities and love me anyway. Heart Sisters who aren't related to me by blood but instead by the sisterly bond entwined between our hearts.

Heart Sisters are just as strong as—and in some cases even stronger than—blood sisters. May we find them and hold on to them always. I know you will, friend.

Love,
Natalie Snapp

INTRODUCTION

You should probably know that I'm not a psychologist, and I haven't been to seminary. I don't have any capital letters following my last name to denote an advanced degree; in fact, I've only completed four years of college finished far longer ago than I care to admit.

However, perhaps Mark Twain said it best when he stated, "A man who carries a cat by the tail learns something he can learn no other way."

I've carried the cat by the tail. Several times. I'm a slow learner, sisters.

While I may not have an official pedigree when it comes to the psychology of women, I am one. Before then, I was a girl, so the female heart is one I've been around for as long as I can remember. My guess is if you are reading this, you know the female heart well, too.

Five years ago, God called me to serve on a leadership team of a ministry consisting of roughly seventy-five women. Two years later, He called me to take the reins and lead it.

During this time, there were definitely moments in which I carried the cat by the tail. However, toward the end of my time as the leader of this group, I had learned how to gently pick up the cat and lean her against my chest. I'm certainly not Jesus, and I still make mistakes in my relationships; however, I've learned a thing or two since those days when I went for the tail.

Fortunately, I was able to walk through several conflicts within one year; though admittedly, it was one of the most difficult years of my life. While I wouldn't choose to go back and do it all over again, I am beyond thankful for the pruning He did in me during this time, and I now see there was no other way to get there.

Nothing worth having is ever easy, and my experience with female relationships and friendships is no different.

There I sat with tears streaming down my face on a cold, winter morning in January. I was in yet another conflict with someone I thought was a friend. I pleaded with God to make it all stop, to make the hurt I kept experiencing from other women just go away. I told God I would never, ever interact with women again and I would steer clear of female friends because I just wasn't very good at this friendship thing. I told myself my husband was enough, and I wouldn't need female friendships because I planned to lose myself in raising my children. I would go it alone because it was simply just too painful to have girlfriends.

But deep down, I knew I needed girlfriends. My husband can't, and shouldn't be expected to, fill the holes only girlfriends can fill.

Many tears were shed as I struggled to repair my broken heart—and the heartbreak I inflicted on others.

I am one imperfect woman, sisters, but oh, how I've learned through His mercy and grace.

Perhaps you are or have been like me on that cold, January morning. Perhaps you've been wounded by a woman or two and you have had enough. Perhaps you just don't think it's worth it so you've fooled yourself into believing your spouse and children are enough.

I don't write this book from a position of "I've got all the answers" or to share a story with you only to have you say, "Well, good for you! But what about me?" I write this book because I'm right there with you—not spouting off about how much I know but instead walking right next to you, experiencing the same relational difficulties that make those of us who choose to follow Jesus question if we really do or not.

In case you're wondering . . . I did interact with women again. I didn't hole myself up at home and vow to have every emotional need met by my husband and my children (you're welcome, honey). Deep down, I knew God didn't really want me to live without other women in my life, so in due time, I cautiously stuck my toes into the waters of friendship again.

It was the fourth best decision I ever made—just behind following Jesus, marrying Jason, and birthing my three babies. Today, my Heart Sisters help me remember to live by truth, take my kids when I need to go to a doctor's appointment, and encourage me to keep going when I want to stop.

And to think . . . I didn't believe I would ever have close friendships.

My prayer is that the pages of this book will encourage you to work hard for the other women around you. To love them. To cry and laugh and genuinely encourage one another instead of being threatened by the "fleshy" feelings of insecurity, jealousy, or comparison.

Although those emotions are very human and a struggle for most of us at some point in our lives, they are most certainly not from God and He doesn't want you to be held in bondage by any of it. Someone has to be the one to wave the white flag. Let that peace-seeker be you.

On that note, there's a common misconception about peace-makers that is just plain not true. They are thought to be door-mats; people who allow their own needs to take the back burner and lie dormant so they can remain conflict-free. However, in reality, peacemakers are those who sense when something is wrong and strive to honor God through healthy conflict resolution. Peacemakers are peace seekers, not peace stealers!

Walking through conflict in a way that honors God is crucial to Heart Sister relationships because so often we are tempted to run from the relationship instead of working through the hard stuff. But did you know that working through the hard stuff can actually make your friendship even stronger? Chapter 4 introduces The P.E.G. System, which will teach you when and how to **P**ray, **E**xamine, and **G**o talk to a friend when a conflict comes up.

I hope you will find that loving the women around you will give you a taste of true freedom—freedom to accept without condition, freedom to truly love your neighbor as yourself, and freedom to live at peace with those around you.

While this book is focused on how women relate to other women, I think you'll find much of what we discuss is applicable to all relationships—male and female, friendship and familial, and even parent and child.

It's no accident you've picked up this book. There is some-thing in here He wants you to read to either reassure you or prune you or both. The Refiner's Fire is hot, but the results are worth enduring the heat.

Know that I am praying for you as you journey through this, sister. May you experience His peace, holy conviction, and truth as you read these pages.

CHAPTER ONE

BUT DO WE REALLY *NEED* GIRLFRIENDS?

> *The glory of friendship is not the outstretched hand,*
> *nor the kindly smile nor the joy of companionship; it*
> *is the spiritual inspiration that comes to one when he*
> *discovers that someone else believes in him and is*
> *willing to trust him.*
>
> Ralph Waldo Emerson

I've always wanted to have a sister. For as long as I can re-member, I longingly watched the girls who had built-in play-mates to share giggles with in the middle of the night and inside jokes about Uncle Harry at family reunions. As an only child, I would have taken a brother as well, but a sister? Oh, the desire of my heart was strong. In fact, I still find myself feeling like an outsider looking in to blood-sister relationships during those moments when I forget I do indeed have sisters—though not by blood.

Through His grace, God granted me those sisters years later. No, we don't have a shared childhood and we don't have inside jokes during family reunions. However, we do have heart

connections that only sisters can have, and the love I possess
for these women rivals the love I have for my husband and
children. You mess with one of my sisters and the pit bull of my
usually even-keeled self starts to smack its jowls.

After becoming a follower of Christ when I was twenty-seven
years old, I quickly put the pieces together that it is He who creates us as women to be relational beings. Listen, I love my husband something fierce, but let's face it—there are some things
the men in our lives are just not going to understand. And who
are we kidding? They don't *want* to understand everything.

During our newlywed years, I told my husband more than
he ever wanted to hear. I gave him the whole book when what
he really wanted was the summary on the back cover. I lost him
early and found myself offended when he only listened to 70
percent of the story because I wanted 100 percent of his attention. Similarly, my husband understands why our two young
sons, who are fifteen months apart, have the desire to catapult
themselves off the top bunk of their beds because he once was
a young boy who wanted to do the same thing. He is; therefore,
he knows. Meanwhile, my daughter and I look on, befuddled
yet accepting that we'll never quite understand, while at times
the boys look at us in the same way.

Now, let's change the scenario to one of my closest friends
and me in a booth at our favorite Mexican joint munching on
chips and salsa and talking over the same situation I shared
with my husband. Invariably, my friend wants to hear more of
the story. She might ask guiding questions or offer solutions or
points to ponder from a female perspective because women
typically get other women. This doesn't mean our husbands
don't "get" us—there's just a different level of understanding

between two women who both know what it's like to have lost yourself amid the diapers and feedings or the carpooling or the pressure to balance it all. Don't get me wrong—our husbands can also be incredibly insightful and sensitive to our thoughts and feelings. I'm in no way bashing the male species.

However, the truth of the matter is we need other women in our tribe. We need to lean on one another and hold each other up when it feels like we can't walk. We need someone to lovingly tell us we should apologize to our spouses when we're in the wrong. We need someone to speak up if the dark brown lipstick makes us look like a corpse. Simply put, God knew we would need all kinds of relationships to fulfill the desire He placed in each of our hearts to live in community.

When we expect our husbands, or any man for that matter, to fulfill all of our relational needs, we are placing an enormous amount of pressure upon his shoulders. If we keep expecting him to fulfill the role of girlfriend, husband, and in some cases, God, we are setting that man up for failure. It's just not realistic nor is it fair to expect him to be able to meet every one of those needs. (And if you have the courage to read the former sentence out loud to your husband, tell him I said "you're welcome.")

So let's consult the Bible and dig around a bit, shall we? Evidence of women-as-relaters is found throughout the Bible beginning with the creation of Eve. God created Adam but soon realized there was "no suitable helper" (Genesis 2:20). After placing Adam in a deep sleep, God created Eve from one of Adam's ribs and he awoke to find the bone of his bone and the flesh of his flesh. No small feat, and of course, he suddenly had the suitable helper he needed. If only it were always so simple, eh?

Eve was created to commune with Adam. The mother of us all was made from his very being to interact and relate to Adam, the first man on the planet. It's a good thing she seemed to like him—she didn't have much else of a choice! Besides this, she became his "help meet" (Genesis 2:20 KJV) and apparently did so pretty effectively since eventually Cain and Abel were born. There might have been a little dysfunction since Cain eventually killed Abel, but then we can rest assured knowing that even the first family on earth had a little baggage.

There's no way around it, sisters. We are who we are who we are. We can't expect the cat to start barking. We are relationship seekers and we were created to be so.

Ruth refused to leave Naomi. Mary immediately sought Elizabeth after learning she was carrying the Christ child. Esther used her relational understanding to stop the destruction of the Hebrews. The list continues but, suffice it to say, there are several examples of women as relaters throughout the Bible.

However, it's not just the Bible that demonstrates the importance of women as relaters. In a landmark study from UCLA roughly ten years ago, it was discovered that when women feel stressed, their brains release a hormone called oxytocin.[1] Oxytocin makes women want to surround themselves with other women, and this releases even more oxytocin, which has a relaxing effect and makes us think everything might be all right after all.

Left over from a time when humans had to be more aware of their surroundings in order to live, the fight-or-flight response describes our natural inclination to flee the scene if we feel threatened. However, the research that coined this phrase was conducted mostly on men. The same UCLA study referenced above found that women and men actually respond to stress differently. (Which, I might add, I didn't need an official study to know. Throat clear.)

In her book *The Tending Instinct*, Shelley E. Taylor discovered that when women feel stressed, they "tend and befriend."[2] In other words, after a tough day, we like to spend the evening tending to our children and befriending our sisters around us. Let the oxytocin gates open and may the flooding begin, I say. The more oxytocin released, the calmer we feel. Hook me up to an intravenous drip, please.

Our bodies even respond *biologically* when we spend time with girlfriends, thus explaining why a night out with the girls now and then is essential to our sanity. Likely due to the oxytocin release, several studies have found social relationships are helping us to live longer, too. Those who have a strong friendship network find themselves with lowered cholesterol, heart rate, and blood pressure. Harvard University is even in on this as well—in their well-respected *Nurses' Health Study*, they discovered that a woman without a network of friends posed a risk to her health that was comparable to smoking or carrying around extra weight.[3] Sobering facts indeed. Girlfriends are a lifeline we cannot afford to live without.

The Bible not only includes several examples of women as strong and pivotal relational beings but also showcases a few women who chose not to live in such a sisterly manner as well. Leah and Rachel, who were blood sisters nonetheless, lived in a state of constant jealousy and rivalry with one another. Jacob was tricked into marrying Leah, a woman he found unattractive but who was so fertile she bore him six sons and one daughter. Yet Jacob didn't love her in the way he loved her sister, Rachel.

Looking sideways at what others have instead of looking up to God and thanking Him for what He's already given you never leads to anything good.

It was Rachel he wanted all along because she was a knockout of a woman, but get this—she was infertile. In fact, Rachel was so bent on bearing sons for Jacob she offered up her maidservant, Bilhah, who bore him two sons. No wonder the twelve tribes of Israel came from Jacob's lineage—he was one prolific breeder.

Some scholars believe that Leah's "weak eyes" refer to the fact they were likely crossed or disfigured in some way. Though her beauty may not have won her the Miss Israel title, she possessed the good eggs that conceived several sons, which eventually led to six of the tribes of Israel. Rachel wanted nothing more than to bear Jacob sons, and Leah wanted nothing more than to obtain Jacob's love. They both desperately wanted what the other possessed. Looking sideways at what others have instead of looking up to God and thanking Him for what He's already given you never leads to anything good. The story of Jacob's wives was the perfect storm—and to think some people believe the Bible is an outdated history book. This trio's story is juicier than any episode of *Days of Our Lives* I've ever seen; not to mention their dilemma is one that continues among women today.

Another example of strife between women in the Bible is Sarai and Hagar. Like Rachel, Sarai (later renamed Sarah) was unable to conceive a child with her husband, Abram (later renamed Abraham). Also like Rachel, she offered up her maidservant, Hagar, to Abram, who lay with her and conceived a son. Soon after, Hagar began to resent Sarai, and Sarai quickly blamed Abram for putting her in this position. (Can you just picture a befuddled Abram trying to figure this one out?) Evidently, he was ready to wash his hands of this situation as he gave Sarai permission to do as she liked with her maidservant. Sarai's solution was to simply be so horrible to Hagar that the only thing the poor maidservant could do to alleviate this tense situation was to flee her mistress.

And flee she did. Hagar ran, confused and alone and desperate to know what God's plan was for her. God spoke to Hagar while she was retrieving water at a well during her journey, and after instructing her to go back to Sarai with the promise He would give Hagar too many descendents to count, He said:

> You are now with child
>   and you will have a son.
> You shall name him Ishmael,
>   for the LORD has heard of your misery.
>
> He will be a wild donkey of a man;
>   his hand will be against everyone
>   and everyone's hand against him,
> and he will live in hostility
> toward all his brothers.
> (Genesis 16:11-12)

Ishmael later became the patriarch of Islam. The repercussions of a fallen female relationship know no boundaries, and its impact can go further than you ever imagined. I'm pretty sure Sarai had no idea of the generational impact her impatience with God's timing would produce.

And, yes, I know there are women who have been horribly wounded by other women. I understand why some women desire to just be left alone or count only men among their friends. One of my readers, who we'll call Stephanie, confided in me she's only recently had girlfriends because she was betrayed and deeply hurt by a friend while in college. This particular friend shared personal information about Stephanie with others—information that had been shared in confidence and was tender to Stephanie's heart. Doesn't this just make you think of the phrase "with friends like these who needs enemies?"

Stephanie retreated from female relationships and became very selective of whom she would give a glimpse into her vulnerabilities. She became a "surface friend" to many but didn't have any friends who truly knew her heart. Stephanie found women to be catty and petty and preferred the company of men.

However, as we discussed earlier, men are equipped to only go so far into the heart of a woman because at the end of the day, they're not women. Being just one of the guys might work for a little while, but eventually, there are going to be situations where a female heart will desire friendship with other women. Our spouses can't be expected to be our sisters. Luckily, Stephanie was able to work through this past hurt, and today has been rewarded with true Heart Sisters who love her and can completely be trusted.

It doesn't help that our culture seems to glorify and profit from catty behavior either. The whole "Real Housewives of Wherever" series is fraught with behavior between women that actually encourages us to live in strife with one another. In fact, the cattier and more disrespectful the behavior among the women on these types of programs, the higher the network ratings. It's true that a story of conflict naturally piques our interest as those disabled by the flesh, but what would happen if we just simply refused to watch shows like "The Real Housewives of Wherever"?

If we waste our time being catty instead of caring, we are extinguishing the light the Holy Spirit illuminates within us.

As followers of Jesus, it's our responsibility to monitor what we allow to enter our hearts. If we do indulge in a guilty pleasure, balancing it out with what is true, noble, pure, and just will keep our hearts centered on God. Television, books, magazines, and websites impact us more than we know. It's our job to guard our hearts *above all else*, and this includes monitoring what we allow into our souls. Caring is always better than catty.

If we waste our time being catty instead of caring, we are extinguishing the light the Holy Spirit illuminates within us. While teaching the Sermon on the Mount in Matthew 5, Jesus talked to the crowd around Him about being the salt and the light. He often taught in parables, stories told with a simple lesson or moral. These intentional parables always had a specific focus, and Jesus knew the direction He was heading and the lessons He wanted His listeners to glean. I admit to being a bit befuddled when I first read about the salt and the light because come on . . . I can purchase salt in a cylinder at my local grocery store for about a dollar. How valuable is that?

Turns out, very. In ancient times, salt was thought to be extremely rare and quite valuable. It was often used as currency, was the culprit of a few conflicts, and according to Homer, was a "divine substance."[4] Salt was set apart. Precious. Not to mention there are more uses for salt than just seasoning our food or melting the ice on our roads. In fact, the salt industry claims fourteen thousand different uses for these small pieces of the only consumable rock in existence.[5] Salt can be used to remove stains from clothing, brighten up the colors of vegetables, seal cracks, extinguish grease fires, and kill poison ivy, to name a few.

In other words, salt is not only precious and valuable. It's useful. And we're called to be the "salt and the light"—which means *we* are precious, valuable, and useful.

Salt also naturally brings out better flavor in what we eat and preserves food from spoiling; therefore, we are to bring out the better flavor in others and keep them from spoiling. In this way, we are useful to God. In the NET Bible, Jesus tells us, "You are the salt of the earth. But if salt loses its flavor, how can it be made salty again? It is no longer good for anything except to be thrown out and trampled on by people" (Matthew 5:13). Is it just me or does this make you a little concerned about losing your flavor? And yes, there are days in which I feel like I've lost my flavor. There are certainly moments when I feel as if God might want to throw me out. Luckily, God's grace covers those less-than-favorable moments.

So we're called to be the salt, which means we are to be set apart. We're precious, valuable, and useful. But we're also called to be the light. Like salt, there is a certain power in light we so often take for granted. Light allows us to function after the sun goes down. It makes scary moments feel not as frightening when it's turned on. It produces a comforting glow. Figuratively, light illuminates the secrets we want to keep in the darkness, so the enemy can't prowl around them anymore. Light is powerful, illuminating, reduces fear, and encourages truth.

It's a bit of a tall order, sisters. If we're called to be the salt and the light, then we're asked to be set apart, precious, valuable, useful, powerful, illuminating, fear-reducing, and truth-seeking. As Jesus shares, "You are the light of the world. A city located on a hill cannot be hidden. People do not light a lamp and put it under a basket but on a lampstand, and it gives light to all in the house. In the same way, let your light shine before people, so that they can see your good deeds and give honor to your Father in heaven" (Matthew 5:14-16 NET).

Let your light shine, sisters. Don't dim it because of fear or because you're worried about someone else's insecurity or are too worried about what others will think of you. Allowing your light to shine is a true example of loving your neighbor as yourself. Loving the women in your life through your sincere and loving light is what Jesus asks us to do. Shine bright.

Now that we've reviewed this background a bit, here's where guarding our hearts is relevant: the eyes are the lamp of the body. We draw light into ourselves through our eyes, and the light that shines out to the world comes from the same place. Therefore, what we allow our eyes, or our lamps, to see is going to affect the kind of light that illuminates those around us—and usually without us even realizing it's happened. What goes in certainly does come out, and unfortunately, I know this from experience.

Years ago, I spent a few months only reading *People* magazine and the latest bestsellers. I would not have dreamed of missing the weekly episode of *The Bachelor*, and I wasn't keeping up with my typical daily reading of the Bible. Soon, I found myself thinking catty thoughts about other women.

Camaraderie was replaced by competition as I began to look at the exterior instead of the heart. I even began to compare my very boring life to those in magazines, books, and television. So I can't help wondering what I am subconsciously illuminating to the world around me if I watch television shows that encourage cattiness among women. How does the media influence how I treat women in my sphere of influence?

Recently, I've been drawn to the book of Matthew, and since I'm using a relatively new translation called The Voice in conjunction with the New International Version, I am discovering connections between Scriptures I haven't seen in the past. In The Voice translation, Matthew 7:13-14 tells us

> there are two paths before you;
> you may take only one path. One
> doorway is narrow. *And one door*
> *is wide.* Go through the narrow
> door. For the wide door leads to
> a wide path, and the wide path
> is broad; the wide, broad path is
> easy, and the wide, broad, easy
> path has many, many people
> on it; but the wide, broad, easy,
> crowded path leads to death.
> The narrow door leads to a nar-
> row road that in turn leads to life.
> It is hard to find that road. Not
> many people manage it.

Not many people manage it because it's far easier to walk the wide path the world so freely offers. However, if we choose to take the narrow path and learn about Jesus, the narrow is suddenly more enticing. I'm not suggesting that trials and heartbreak are suddenly erased once we start to walk the narrow path, but as a hammer helps us pound nails into a board, the narrow path gives us the tools we need to stay on the narrow path. Shoot your arrow toward the narrow path and hide from the wide.

Matthew 22:37-40 tells us that the first and greatest commandment is to love God with all our hearts, souls, and minds. The second is to simply love your neighbor as yourself. Every single teaching in the New Testament is based on these two—one called the "Great Commandment" and the other the "Great Commission." There's something about that word "commandment" that makes me think we should probably just do it. Likewise, when we commission someone, we hire that person. We've been hired by God to do the specific job of loving others as ourselves. Jesus didn't suggest we choose to follow these two principles, and He didn't ask if we wanted to do so. He commanded and commissioned it. He's not messing around with these two.

To shoot our arrow toward the narrow path, we need to choose to love God above all else and then choose to love those around us as ourselves. Choosing to love the women around us and desire good for them is an example of loving our neighbors as ourselves. We rejoice when they rejoice and we weep when they weep (Romans 12:15).

We are all broken. Every last one of us. Each of us has days in which we are ministering to others and days when we are being ministered to. He wants us to be in the game. He needs us to show up and be the hands and feet of His son. It's our job.

What could happen if we started a revolution of love, support, and sisterhood among women? How much freedom would we feel if we gave each other the benefit of the doubt and chose relationship instead of conflict? Would our hearts break less if we chose to work through those conflicts in humility instead of running away and adding more layers to the scars? Would we fight the inappropriate media that stereotypes us as catty and against one another and force it to stop? Would extramarital affairs even exist if women agreed to stand together as sisters? The power we have as women is staggering.

We need someone to share in our laughter. Sometimes we need a good cry with a sister by our side. Other times, we need her to carry us because we simply don't think we can put one foot in front of the other on our own. We need Heart Sisters.

DISCUSSION QUESTIONS

1. Why do you feel like you need girlfriends? Journal or share in a group.

2. What makes a good friend?

3. Have you ever had a conversation with your significant other or any male figure in your life and realized that it might be best to be saved for female ears? Why do you think this happens?

4. Have you ever found yourself in a position of expecting your significant other to be your everything? Why might this be difficult for him or her? On the other hand, have you ever felt as if someone wanted you to be his or her everything? If so, how did it make you feel?

5. Which example of friendship from the Bible resonates with you the most? Why?

CHAPTER TWO

GET RIGHT WITH GOD,
GET RIGHT WITH OTHERS

'Cause I want to get right with God. Yes, you know you got to get right with God.

Lucinda Williams

It had been a busy season of writing, and I was struggling to keep all the plates in my life spinning. Between hours spent on my laptop, my three children's school and activity schedules, and managing a home, time with God quickly went by the wayside. I wasn't taking time to rest and recharge and soon found myself navigating each day on autopilot.

I noticed my fuse shortening when I interacted with those I loved the most. I got irritated with girlfriends over things that were not a big deal, and I am pretty certain my husband would tell you he wasn't enjoying being married to me. Thank God for the vows of "For better or for worse!"

It's hard to keep our relationships in sync when our relationship with God is out of sync. I know this from experience—I would like to tell you I'm a girl that's put her hand on a hot stove only once and never repeated the same mistake again;

but alas, I would be lying. Of course, the language is figurative but the truth in my confession of being drawn to the heat is not.

It took me a long while to discover that no other relationships in my life were going to be healthy or good before my relationship with the Lord was healthy and good. Reading a book about Christian female friendships without first getting on the right path with Jesus is like staring at the dots of paint in a Pointillist painting without ever seeing the scope of the entire masterpiece. There is some background information we need to know before we can see the whole work, and the same is true with relationships—until we "get right with God" we'll continue to spin our relational wheels and live with frustration and confusion. It's not a someday-I'll-commit-to-spending-more-time-with-Him type of thing, sisters. It wasn't until I made my relationship with Jesus the number one priority above all else that I began to realize my other relationships were lacking a certain depth I didn't even know I was missing.

When I began to walk closer with God, I started to internalize His truth. I once talked and expected God to listen, but now I know the more I listen, the more He talks. I've finally learned to discern who is leading and who is not. I slowly began to remove the reins from my hands, and over time, I passed them to God— who's been waiting for them since He created my inmost being. I won't say I don't ever try to rip the reins back from His hands, but the humility I've learned from submitting to His will has been the missing piece of the relationship puzzle. Most importantly, I'm learning it's just not all about me—and it never has been.

A few nights ago, some of my friends and I were discussing Matthew 19:24 about the camel fitting through the eye of a needle. If you aren't familiar with this verse, Jesus is responding to the man who asked what else he could do to best follow Jesus. He lived an honorable life and seemed to desire a closer relationship with Jesus, but when he was told to sell all of his belongings and follow Jesus, he was saddened. He was a rich man and ridding himself of his material possessions was more than he was willing to sacrifice. He wanted to keep a tight grip on his baggage—his *things* were more important than radically following Jesus. And yes, this passage makes me squirm in my chair a bit.

"I tell you the truth, it will be hard for a rich person to enter the kingdom of heaven! Again I say, it is easier for a camel to go through the eye of a needle than for a rich person to enter into the kingdom of God" (Matthew 19:23-24 NET), Jesus tells His disciples as the man dejectedly walks away. I admit, until my friends and I had this discussion, this had been a verse I glossed over. I remember scratching my head and wondering what on earth was meant by this odd comparison. Nonetheless, I arrived at the conclusion Jesus was merely trying to communicate the impossibility of a rich man entering heaven. A camel could never fit through the eye of a needle. Not even on its skinny days.

However, Jesus wasn't speaking on a concrete, obvious level. He was speaking in a manner than was culturally relevant and relatable to His listeners. Back in the day, it was common for a city to be surrounded by a high wall. The entrance to the city was marked by a large gate open during the day with a much smaller gate for use after hours. This small gate was called the "eye of the needle," and the only way a camel could pass through was if all of its bags were removed and it crawled through on its knees.

If we want to get right with God, it isn't going to happen until we are willing to pass through the eye of the needle. However, we're going to have to follow the camel's lead: we must go on our knees in humility, shedding the bags that weigh us down so we can fit through that small opening. Humility is essential if we are ever going to go higher up and deeper in with God. In fact, humility is the essential element to a closer relationship with Jesus—*and* others.

Maybe you're like the rich man and you would just rather hold on to your stuff. Or maybe you're like I once was and the thought of stripping your baggage grips you with a fear that seems completely illogical and invokes instant panic because it can be painful. Or maybe you're a little bit of both. It is sometimes difficult to consider parting with our stuff (both literal and figurative) because after all, isn't it who we are? Doesn't the stuff we've walked through make us who we are? What about the hurt that could surface when we begin to take those bags off our backs?

It's been thirteen years since I started to unload my own bags, and I'm still under construction. However, this I have learned: carrying the heavy weight of emotional baggage is far more painful than the freedom found in laying them down. It did hurt at times, yes. There were days I wasn't having much fun unpacking them; but then, I'm not sure we're supposed to be having fun every single moment of our lives. Sometimes we have to wade through the junk that's just plain hard, the junk that's attached itself to us and whispered lies about God and who we are in His eyes. That junk doesn't tell the truth, sisters. It gets its life from holding on to you, and it doesn't want to be released because then it loses its power to influence. But take heed—there's hope. The momentum of those lies halts once a relationship with Jesus is strengthened. Nothing fights lies more effectively than truth.

What are some of those lies we women believe? What keeps us from embracing authentic female friendships or any other type of relationship for that matter? Unfortunately, there are many lies we hear louder than truth; however, let's focus on the ones that make up the "Fearless Five" by using the phrase "Can't Ever Imagine Being Friends":

1. Comparison: Aye-yi-yi! This one is brutal. I've seen so many friendships either disintegrate or never even transpire due to the sneaky lie of comparison. Unfortunately, it seems to plague women more than it does men. We compare our hair color or the size of our jeans or our homes or the performance of our children or you name it. Sadly enough, we begin to see everyone through a very distorted lens not based in reality! When we compare, we put ourselves down and the reality of others' lives up.

For example, my house is oftentimes a train wreck. I don't want it to be a train wreck. In fact, I despise clutter and desire organization. However, in this season of my life, with three young children and a spouse that has a demanding schedule, I've accepted that there is going to be a certain measure of clutter in my home. I can easily clean it up well when guests are expected, but if you stop by unannounced, just be prepared to find Legos strewn on the kitchen table and socks, well, everywhere.

When I walk through the door of a very organized, free-of-clutter home with the scent of vanilla sugar cookie candles hanging in the air and soft jazz looping on the iPod, I can't help but compare. My home is not the sanctuary I want it to be, and while I realize my expectations are probably not very realistic and to aspire to reach this lofty standard while in this particular season of life would drive me insane, I still compare. I get home and assess the damage and view everything through a more critical eye than when I left. I might go into a rant about how I'm the only one who ever does anything around the house and why on earth can't we just pick up the Magna-Tiles? When I compare myself to others, my blood pressure increases and the woman I want to be decreases.

> *When I compare myself to others, my blood pressure increases and the woman I want to be decreases.*

Comparison takes me down roads I don't want to travel. It boils ingratitude to the surface and encourages me to look at what I don't have rather than what I do. Comparisons breathe death and steal joy and they're born when we look sideways at others instead of looking up to God.

Not to mention when we compare, we are oftentimes unknowingly putting down the work of the Creator Himself. He knit us together in our mothers' wombs and tells us we are fearfully and wonderfully made (Psalm 139:13-14). He knows how many hairs are on each of our heads (Luke 12:7; Matthew 10:30). He tells us we are His (Isaiah 43:1). He thinks pretty highly of YOU. And yes, He thinks highly of HER as well, but YOU are the only one that can fulfill the purpose He intended for you to execute. Only YOU. Even when He is the artist of you both.

One of my favorite passages in the Bible is when Jesus returns after His crucifixion and visits Simon Peter in John 21. You may remember that Peter was the one who denied knowing Jesus three times, and Jesus being Jesus, He wanted to go back and give Peter the chance to make things right again. After asking Peter if he loves Him three different times, Jesus then goes on to foretell to Peter a few details of his future death. Peter answers with "Master, what's going to happen to *him*?" meaning John. Jesus said, "If I want him to live until I come again, what's that to you? You—follow me" (John 21:21-22 *THE MESSAGE*).

Seven often overlooked powerful words in the Bible: "What's that to you? You—follow me." I love Peter. He was a man very much disabled by the flesh—filled with many foibles and mis-steps—yet Jesus loved him so much. I can't tell you how many times I've visualized myself as Peter, walking behind Jesus and comparing myself to the people around me—the people I see when I look sideways. Without fail, roughly twenty seconds into the thought, I hear those seven words and I'm reminded of who I follow and where to look—up, not sideways.

We all bring unique gifts and talents to the table of life, sisters. We can't have everything. I would love to be able to sing on a stage and lead people in worship, but it's not my gifting area, and it's not how God wants me to serve. He did, however, gift my friends Melinda and Shelly with musical ability, and I am blessed to delight in their talents often. My friend Katrina is a wonderful speaker and is one of those annoying people who actually likes to exercise. Dana is an incredible leader and runs a ministry in Africa. Rachel was created to mother six children and does so beautifully. Laurie can remember details like no one I've ever seen. My other sister Rachel is a wise soul with great depth and shares a very close relationship with God. If I allowed the spirit of comparison to reach in and yank the possibility of becoming close friends with any of these women away, my life would be devoid of the rich blessings they have all brought to my life.

2. Envy: "Mom, what does *jealous* mean?" my four-year-old asked from the backseat of our minivan. "It means you are scared you're going to lose something to someone else," I

replied. "I want Samuel's car. Does this mean I'm jealous?" he asked, brown eyes serious and brow furrowed. "No, it means you are envious. You envy Samuel because of his car—you want the car, so you feel envy," I clarified. "Yes, I have envy for Samuel," he confirmed. I chuckled because envy boils to the surface so early in our lives, doesn't it? The flesh disables us all and causes us to respond from its constraints rather than from the freedom of truth. Comparison and envy can eat away the soul quicker than battery acid on skin. It destroys the flesh and burrows within, and there you are, standing with holes in your skin and wounds that run deep.

If comparisons breathe death, then envy is the cancer that consumes the soul. In fact, the English Standard Version of Proverbs 14:30 reads, "A tranquil heart gives life to the flesh, but envy makes the bones rot." Bone-rotting envy chews up your dreams, gulps down your own unique gifts, and spits out the carnage so it looks a bit like who you once were, but inside, you've been derailed. And it doesn't come from God. Ever.

Everyone has a story that is uniquely his or her own. God invites us to partake in individual journeys and allows us to experience joy, trauma, sadness, and love. My story is just that: mine. Your story is, well, yours. Our stories are not the same, and thank God! How boring would that be? What matters is that we arrive at the same destination—at the foot of the cross. So as Heart Sisters, let's choose to celebrate each other's strengths and marvel at the source of their creation. James 1:17 tells us that every good and perfect gift is from above, and so often, what we envy is something good and perfect. We are envying gifts that come from Him. If you look hard enough, you'll find you're abundantly blessed by good, perfect, and *different*.

3. Insecurity: Comparison and envy conspire together to deride our identity, and before we know it, we've become a shell of uncertainty. Insecure. Lacking in confidence. Remember when we talked about being disabled by the flesh? One of our flesh tendencies is to be a little self-absorbed. While it's true some are more self-absorbed than others, all of us suffer from this affliction to a degree. Now, take this natural tendency and add it to a culture that tends to stress "It's all about me." In fact, our culture stresses this so much that I've seen young girls wearing it on T-shirts! When we believe it's all about us and we see something enticing that belongs to someone else, be it a new car or a lot of friends or a beautiful, big home (clutter-free, of course), we compare. If we compare too much, it's likely we will begin to be envious. Too much comparison and envy will eventually destroy our security and attempt to rock the roots of even the most firmly planted people.

In a culture that encourages more, more, and more and leads us to believe it is all about us, we face a steep challenge. But it's not an impossible challenge, sisters. Talking about our own insecurities brings what the enemy would like you to keep in the dark out into the light, where God can do His best healing work. Vulnerability gives others a glimpse into our hearts and communicates an authenticity that tears down the wall that veils who you really are. C. S. Lewis once said, "Friendship is born at that moment when one person says to another 'What! You too? I thought I was the only one.'" There is reassurance in knowing you aren't alone.

The best way to fight insecurity can be learned from the apostle Paul. In 2 Corinthians, Paul discusses the thorn he was given from Satan to keep him from becoming conceited. (Scholars are unsure of what Paul's thorn actually was.) He pleaded with God to remove this thorn, but God wouldn't do it. "My grace is sufficient for you, for my power is made perfect in your weakness," he reassures Paul (2 Corinthians 12:9). This is one of my favorite verses in the Bible because in the end, His grace IS enough. However, many commentaries on this chapter will stop here. Yet in the remainder of verse 9 through verse 10, Paul says, "I will boast all the more gladly about my weaknesses, so that Christ's power may rest on me. That is why, for Christ's sake, I delight in weaknesses, in insults, in hardships, in persecutions, in difficulties. For when I am weak, then I am strong."

According to Paul, we must (1) accept that each of us possesses thorns that won't be removed and must rely on Him for strength, (2) grow our roots deeper in the ways He works and the words of His truth, and (3) talk about our junk. He *delights* in his weaknesses, sisters. I don't know about you, but it's a rare occasion when I feel delighted to have to deal with my heavy baggage. I certainly don't delight in insults. I'm not dying to experience another hardship anytime soon, and persecution and difficulty are not high on my priority list.

Yet here's Paul, considered to be the greatest apostle of all time, letting his guard down and being vulnerable with us. He tells of his insecurities and shares his struggles. He leans into truth, and he even boasts about these thorns so God's redemption and grace can be the focus and not his own sad story. Our insecurities are not ours to clutch tightly and proclaim, "Woe is me!" They're tools used to convey God's greatness to others.

4. Being prideful: We could just spend the rest of this book discussing the commonality and pitfalls of pride, now, couldn't we? Pride is an incredibly sneaky relationship-destroyer, and I

> *Vulnerability is a product of humility, and humility is the foundation of a healthy relationship.*

didn't even realize it affected me until I really started to learn more about its true definition. There once was a time when I thought of pride as simply bragging too much or having a higher confidence than what matched reality; however, as I began to really study the Scriptures, I learned that pride is actually the foundation of so many ills in the world—and it's rooted in fear.

Pride is the stubborn mule that makes us believe *they* should apologize to us because we've done nothing wrong. It's also responsible for tricking its victims into believing that once someone has wounded them, that particular someone doesn't deserve the benefits of reconciliation even if the offender is humble and seeks forgiveness. I like to call pride the great thief because it steals relationships, personal growth, and joy—just to name a few. It prides itself on its sneaky style and infiltrates around our very being by the ways of the world and the lies we are led to believe.

While the above are obvious examples of pride, the discovery of its more nonchalant ways were the catalyst that opened my eyes to my own issues with pride. Pride is essentially the fear of being revealed that we don't actually have it all together or figured out. It's an air that's put on to distract others from knowing us authentically and blocks our ability to be vulnerable. Vulnerability is a product of humility, and humility is the foundation of a healthy relationship. Therefore, we can conclude if vulnerability results from humility and humility is the foundation of relationships, then the ability to be vulnerable is pretty essential to achieving meaningful relationships with others.

When we refuse to accept help, especially when we really need it, we are the victims of pride. When we overschedule ourselves because we've said yes to too much, it's oftentimes because we think we are the only ones who can do the tasks and do them well—and yes, this is pride, too. When we tirelessly minister to someone at the expense of our families and grow frustrated when that person doesn't act the way we think he or she should, we are the victims of pride. We can't be Jesus to anyone. Only Jesus can be Jesus. The only role we play is to fulfill what we've been called to do then sit back and allow the Holy Spirit to do what only the Holy Spirit can do.

The best way to combat pride is to humble ourselves—first to God, then to others. Like Paul, if we choose to reveal our weaknesses, we show our humanity and the power of God both. It's necessary to talk about our thorns. Admit we don't know everything or have it all together or live in a state of perfection. Give ourselves permission to be vulnerable, especially to God. He is fully aware of our struggles, disappointments, and hurts, so revealing these to Him won't be anything He doesn't already know.

However, when we cry out to the Lord about what breaks our hearts, we humble ourselves to Him. We invite Him into these issues—exactly what He desires. In the fourth chapter of James, we are told "God opposes the proud, but gives grace to the humble" (v. 6 ESV). In other words, He's not so happy with those of us who allow our pride to have a front seat within our soul. I don't know about you, but I need His grace more than anything else because I mess up a lot. If grace is the reward we receive when we humble ourselves to our Creator, then sign me up!

Once I was able to fully humble myself to the Lord, something funny began to happen with my own personal relationships—I was able to more freely humble myself to others. Perhaps it was because I finally began to understand the meaning of humility, or maybe it was because when we humble ourselves, we give the Holy Spirit more access to our souls. Regardless, God wants us to bring all of it, every last ugly bit of our flesh, to the light. If we keep it in the darkness, the enemy has control and will do further damage. It's only when we bring our junk to the light that Jesus can do His best work of healing because He redeems it all. Of course, this doesn't mean our lives suddenly become easy. But it does mean we will have a firm foundation when the hardships come again or the lies threaten to creep back into the inner workings of our minds. If we redirect our self-pride to pride in the Lord, then we must accept help, reveal weaknesses, and give others a chance to take on tasks because it's only then God receives the glory. Self-pride glorifies the flesh while God-pride glorifies His ways—His perfect and flawless ways (Psalm 18:30).

5. Fear: If pride and lack of humility are the culprits behind dissolving relationships, then we can trace their roots back to the foot of fear. So many stems sprout from the seeds of fear. Anxiety. Depression. Pride. Worry. Self-doubt. These stems continue to grow and sprout new branches, and before we even know it, they've begun to vine themselves around our health, our relationships, and our spiritual beliefs.

Fear can also be deceptively sneaky because we don't always know when we're scared. It also has the power to take away our true selves and replace them with false selves—who we become when we're fearful. Those who are preoccupied with outward appearances are scared of being revealed as imperfect. Those with anxiety are scared of the unknown. People who are always tough and wearing armor are often petrified of showing vulnerability because they think it's a weakness. Those who won't accept help and insist on doing everything themselves are fearful of relinquishing control and cannot humble themselves enough to ask for help. And those who must always be the center of attention are often scared of being rejected and feel as though they must perform to be loved.

See how so many negative emotions can be traced back to the root of fear? I can quickly move into an I'll-Do-It-Myself mode when I'm overwhelmed and become a martyr because I can be scared to ask for help. As the mother of three young children and the wife of a man whose occupation often calls him away, I often find the tasks on my list to be overwhelming. Add this to too little sleep, arguing children, and incomplete homework and it's possible I just might slip into my false self. If I do, I'll often lament how I'm the only one who can do anything. How no one can be bothered to set the table. How I'm so tired because my tasks are too many and no one is willing to lend a hand and on and on and on. I become the clanging gong from 1 Corinthians 13—even I can't stand the sound of my own voice.

When I slip into my false self, I ask myself this question: "Natalie, what are you afraid of?" I then work backwards, one step at a time, to determine what has led me to this point. I'm afraid of not having it all together and being unorganized. I'm tired and I'm fearful I won't ever get to sleep because there's too much to be done. I'm scared I won't get any time to myself to unwind and regroup before it starts all over again tomorrow.

And all of this fear traces back to . . . pride. I am not superwoman, and the only person who expects me to be is me. I've left God out of the equation, allowed my Martha tendencies to surface, and handed over control to fear instead of faith.

How do we kick fear in the teeth and command it to go away? For so many of us, it will involve time and grace with ourselves. The first step is always to pray. Ask God to reveal ways in which you are being controlled by fear and how it is affecting your relationships and general well-being. Secondly, increasing our awareness of our fears by asking ourselves the question, "What am I afraid of?" when we feel ourselves becoming anxious, depressed, or worried can assist us in being intentional with decreasing the power of fear. When we identify these triggers, we can then partner with God to let the healing begin and learn how to operate in the true, redeemed selves we were created to be. There will be days in which we'll forget, and that's OK—if God gives us grace, surely we can give ourselves grace, too!

So now that we've identified a few lies that keep us from being close to God, let's take a look at what we can do to "get right with Him" so we can not only live a fulfilled life of walking closer with our Father but also experience healthier relationships with others. As I'm writing this, I feel the need to emphasize that in no way do I have this all figured out, sisters. I'm not preaching to you from the pulpit or telling you all about the great things I've done, only to have you say, "Good for you," at the end of this book. I'm sharing this with you as someone who is right there with you, walking through this journey of faith and learning each day what it really means to follow Jesus.

When I slip into my false self, it's time for me to "get right with God." There's something unsteady and it's time to refocus. Here's how I get back on track:

1. **"Quiet" Time with God:** I place quotations around the word *quiet* because I think so many of us are intimidated by this phrase. Quiet time. Whenever I hear this, I feel a bit of frustration boil to the surface. So often, we're taught that quiet time with the Lord must be done a certain way, at a specific time of the day, and must include certain elements in an exact order. Blech. I'm sorry but this just makes me feel like I'm adding one more thing to check off on my list, you know? Here's the thing: the point of quiet time with God is to commune with Him through His word. As long as you are doing this, there are no right or wrong ways to do quiet time.

2. **Worship:** While worship is about God and not us, there is no doubt in my mind He speaks to us through song. It's highly intimate. I can worship God with any song; however, it's true there are some styles of music that encourage engagement more than others. I'm not at all suggesting we make worship about our needs and what we desire—the point of worship is to exalt him, and this can be done in the format of traditional hymns or contemporary worship songs. However, I do think there are some types of music that touch us more deeply than others, and it's important to discover what appeals to you. Your worship of Him will be enhanced and if you're like me, you'll find your personal relationship with God growing that much deeper.

Give yourself the freedom to worship however you feel led to worship. If you want to raise your hands, do it. If you don't feel the need to worship with hands in the air, don't. This isn't about anyone else but God—you're not performing. At the same time, I want to encourage you to not be inhibited by those around you and instead enjoy this time exalting and praising a God who pours an abundant amount of blessings over His followers.

3. **Prayer:** The best way to develop any relationship is to nurture it through conversation. When we talk to God, we are communing with Him, and this talking leads to a kindling of our relationship. Prayer is talking to God, and it doesn't have to be formal or spoken through a middleman. Each of us has a direct line! God wants us to engage with Him and rejoices when we turn to Him first and foremost. While I don't want to suggest there is a correct or incorrect way to pray (there's not), I tend to follow the A.C.T.S. acronym: Adoration, Confession, Thanksgiving, and Supplication. However, there are also times during the day when I send up a quick prayer to intercede in the events of the day or offer thanks for something that has happened. I ask for patience on more occasions than I care to admit!

Breath prayers are also a way to grow closer to God by consistently praying a short and simple prayer that centers us when needed. For example, my breath prayer as of late has been "More of you, less of me, Lord." I inhale when I speak "more of you" and exhale at the "less of me"—I'm symbolically breathing Him in and exhaling me.

4. **Go to church:** Yes, I believe you can choose not to attend a church and still have a personal relationship with Jesus. Yet I believe we were designed to live in community, and attending church, be it a traditional church or a home church, can greatly enhance your personal relationship with God. No churches are perfect—I have heard many unfortunate stories of believers who have become like Pharisees and focus more on rules rather than relationships. Churches are led by people who are disabled by the flesh, too. Just because they're in public ministry doesn't mean they have become Jesus! Sin is everywhere—even in church. But we do have a choice as to how we handle that

sin: we can become bitter toward the church body or we can discern what we can learn. After my husband and I experienced a trying time with our former church, we continued to attend for another year. It was then clear God was nudging us to visit other churches, so we obeyed—and the fruit from this change has been such a blessing. There was indeed a time when we were a little turned off by organized religion, yet slowly, we felt as though we were being asked to dip our toe back into the water. And I'm so thankful we did.

5. **Forgive others—and yourself:** One of the biggest roadblocks to our relationship with God and therefore, with others, is unforgiveness. I could spend the rest of this book talking about it; in fact, there are hundreds of books written about forgiveness. When we refuse to forgive, the inevitable conclusion of bitterness and resentment eventually takes root, and when this happens, the resulting fruit is spoiled, poisoned, and biting. I recently ran across the passage from Matthew 7 in which we are told:

> By their fruit you will recognize them. Do people pick grapes from thorn bushes, or figs from thistles? Likewise every good tree bears good fruit, but a bad tree bears bad fruit. A good tree cannot bear bad fruit, and a bad tree cannot bear good fruit. Every tree that does not bear good fruit is cut down and thrown into the fire. Thus, by their fruit you will recognize them. (Matthew 7:16-20)

Ouch. Every time I read this passage, I'm deeply convicted. We will be known by the fruit we produce. And I certainly don't want to be a tree thrown into the fire!

Refusing to forgive poisons our soul with bitterness, resentment, and anger. Eventually, this poison causes us to view everything through a negative lens. Forgiving others does release those who have hurt you from their offense, but forgiveness is really not for them—it's for you. No one is without sin, and refusing to forgive gives the offender a power over your life that only God should have. Not to mention we have been forgiven of so much by God through Jesus, and He expects us to forgive as well.

On another note, some of us have junk we need to forgive of ourselves. Can I get an amen here on this one? When I was twenty-three years old, and well before I was a follower of Jesus, I committed a sin so great I was sure I was disqualified from ever being loved and accepted by God. It wasn't until I chose to follow Him four years later that I began to learn more about His ways, and it became apparent I was carrying around unforgiveness toward myself even after God had released me from the offense. I then realized this was another time in which pride snuck in because if God can forgive me, why can't I forgive myself? Am I mightier than our Creator? Of course not. If He can forgive me, I can forgive myself. This doesn't mean there won't be consequences to our choices, but it does mean we are released by Him, so shouldn't we release ourselves?

6. **Watch your schedule:** OK, sisters. Overscheduling is among the top five reasons why we don't spend time with God, isn't it? Or is this just me? I don't know about you but I'm a recovering Yes Girl. I found I was emptying myself for the sake of ministry. My number one ministry, my sweet family, was suffering. I experienced a turning point when my youngest child flashed his big brown eyes and said, "Mama, will you read me a story?"—but I couldn't because I had too many other ministries

that needed my time. We can fill our schedules up with so much good, can't we?

A few months after this exchange with my son, I called an end to all obligations that didn't involve our little family of five or my writing. Now and then I'll make a meal or commit to helping at my children's schools, but not at the expense of my number one ministry. I can't most effectively minister to my number one ministry if I haven't ministered to myself. It was time to re-center and figure out why on earth I felt as if I needed to say yes to everything in the first place. Guess what? Pride showed up again along with the desire for people to like me. These are issues I needed to process with God, but I couldn't if I was running a million miles a day.

When we are pouring out too much of ourselves by over-scheduling our lives and refusing to incorporate margin, we deplete precious energy. A full calendar leads to an empty cup. We become mentally, physically, and spiritually exhausted. Unfortunately, the ones who suffer are the ones we love the most. However, when I prioritized my own growth and well-being, I suddenly had more than just leftovers for my family. The fruit that bloomed from the abundance was far richer than that which resulted from the leftovers.

Getting right with God is a crucial step before we can get right with anyone else. Like Peter in Matthew 14:30, when we take our eyes off Him, we sink. And so does everything else. We deserve to be in healthy relationships because it's through our interactions with others that we advertise what we stand for—and that's Jesus. I'm praying for us all as we navigate this journey together because we deserve to live the life He's planned for us, sister!

DISCUSSION QUESTIONS

1. Which one of the "Fearless Five" lies resonated the most with you: comparison, envy, insecurity, being prideful, or fear? All of the above? Some of the above?

2. What happens when you operate from your false self rather than your true self? What typically leads you into your false self?

3. What are some things that invoke fear in you? Can you identify ways in which fear might be controlling you?

4. What is something you do right now that deepens your relationship with God? What is something you would like to add to your time with Him?

5. Are you presently overscheduled, and do you have enough margin in your life? If not, what steps can be taken to achieve more margin?

CHAPTER THREE

SEEK AND YOU WILL FIND

The only way to have a friend is to be one.
Ralph Waldo Emerson

Eight years ago, my husband joined a dental practice in
a city about an hour from where we were living. I continued to work as a reading specialist at an elementary
school not far from our home. But after being in the workforce
for one year and paying for infant childcare from a teacher's
salary, it no longer made financial sense for me to work outside
of the home. The one thing tying us to our community was now
gone.

My family was there. Most of my friends were there. I had
job connections and loved our church. Our roots were deep. I
wish I could tell you I accepted my husband's prodding to move
to the city where he was practicing dentistry with grace, but I
didn't. I firmly dug in my heels and resisted even the slightest
possibility of moving so fiercely that God had no choice but to
reveal my own selfishness through an exhausted husband who
arrived home in the evenings just long enough to kiss his baby
daughter good night before he woke up and did it all over

again. It was not the kind of life we wanted for our family. Alas, the move was inevitable.

When I was eight months pregnant with our second child, the moving vans came to haul everything away to a new community where we knew only three or four people at most. I was terrified, and to add insult to injury, our first son was born three weeks early—a mere ten days after the moving vans pulled out of our new driveway. My husband was at a point in the practice buy-in plan where what he personally produced was his paycheck—nothing more, nothing less. For someone who was brand spanking new in the community, this was a tall order. He worked constantly. In fact, he worked so much that he wasn't able to stay in the hospital with me and therefore, picked us up on the morning of our release, drove us home, and then returned to the office. While it was difficult for me, I know it was even more so for him.

Our two-year-old daughter was in the care of my mother, so as my husband pulled out of the driveway to return to work, I sat on the couch in this foreign home that seemed to belong to someone else and just cried. I didn't know a soul, and I needed a girlfriend. While I was blessed by my friends in our old community, it was still an hour away, and they had their own young families that needed attention. For the first time, I began to understand the importance of a network of girlfriends I could do life with on a somewhat daily basis. I was isolated, lonely, and shell-shocked by the transition of not only moving to a new community but also giving birth to our second child in the midst of this big change in our lives.

Although I didn't realize it at the time, God had gifted us in the timing of our move because it was late spring. Neighbors began to come out of hibernation, and we quickly discovered many of us had children of the same age. We began to create community, and I started to feel less isolated. Even then, I still longed for girlfriends who would "get" me, friends with whom I could communicate with just a glance. I concluded I was being unfair because my closest friend and I were this way and perhaps I was basing my expectations for new friendships on a relationship that was years deep.

While there is some truth to the comfort level of a years-old friendship, I soon discovered there are many factors that contribute to the development of a sisterhood, and in some cases, this development can happen rather quickly. All friendship relationships start somewhere, right? During the summer months following our spring move, I began to accept the fact that I lived in a new community, and it would be home for the next thirty years at least. I had a choice to make: I could plug in or pull out. Being an extroverted girl who desires community, I knew the pulling-out option wouldn't work for me. Plugging in was my only choice if I was going to do more than just survive in our new city.

I sought out moms' groups. I registered my two-year-old for a twice-weekly preschool. I joined our local Mothers of Preschoolers (MOPS) group. Slowly, I began to put my heart out there for new friendships to take root, and because many of us were in the same season of life, they began to grow.

But before we get into the places where friendships might bloom, let's take a look at the one who was sent to teach us all about relationship: Jesus. God came to Earth as Jesus so (1) we could experience who He really is; (2) He could model His plan for relationships; (3) He could offer healing and redemption;

and (4) He could bridge the gap between God and us. Whenever I feel overwhelmed by the magnitude of my job as a mother, wife, and writer, I try to remember Jesus and His several roles to fulfill, and I am quickly humbled! However, in the end, that's just it—only Jesus, God in the flesh, could pull all of that off perfectly. I personally need some help with it all.

The New Testament is filled with examples of Jesus relating to others. In fact, relationships were at the heart of His ministry. His first commandment is to love God above all else, but His second commandment tells us we must "love our neighbor as ourselves." We can't love without interacting with those we are to love, right? Furthermore, interaction with another always produces a relationship of some kind. It's true that we can show love to a stranger and never see him or her again; however, for that brief moment, there was a "mini" relationship. Even if that relationship doesn't continue past the passing interaction, we had the opportunity to show the love of Christ through a relational opportunity with another person.

Jesus' public ministry was focused on loving others, and although He was controversial to some, others wanted any piece of Him they could get. However, even Jesus had boundaries and put them into place not only out of necessity for His own well-being but also out of compassion. We cannot possibly be emotionally close to thousands of people, but whereas Jesus did possess supernatural abilities, He knew one of His purposes was to model realistic relationships. His love for us was so great that He refused to deviate from the reality of our bound-by-the-flesh capabilities—even when He could have done so.

While Jesus' ministry did not discriminate and was open to all, He did have deeper friendships with a smaller group of people—

His twelve disciples. Closer still were Peter, James, and John, who were considered to be His very best friends. And let's not forget the love He possessed for Mary Magdalene; Martha; Martha's sister, Mary; and their brother, Lazarus. Let's take a look at Jesus' relationships through a graphic organizer that displays the closeness of His friendships:

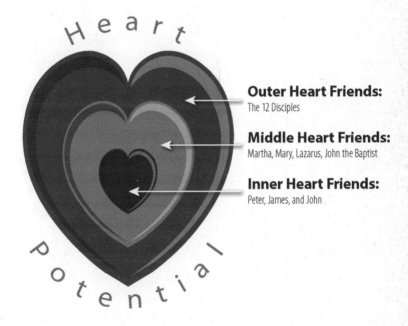

Outer Heart Friends:
The 12 Disciples

Middle Heart Friends:
Martha, Mary, Lazarus, John the Baptist

Inner Heart Friends:
Peter, James, and John

Jesus' "Inner Heart" friends were Peter, James, and John. These were His closest friends He turned to for help, prayer, and love. We'll talk more about them soon, but these were the three Jesus sought first and foremost. They knew His heart and He trusted them greatly. Typically, we might have between two and three "Inner Heart" friends.

·The next heart shows Jesus' "Middle Heart" friends. These would include Mary Magdalene; Martha; Mary (sister of Martha);

their brother, Lazarus; and John the Baptist. These are friends you love as well but just might not be the first two or three people you call upon. However, you are still very vulnerable with your four to six "Middle Heart" friends and you trust and love them greatly.

Next we see "Outer Heart" friends—these are the seven to ten friends you often see socially and consistently spend time with just doing life together. Jesus' disciples were examples of His "Outer Heart" friends. These are the friends who are often in the same season of life, perhaps raising children within the same age range or experiencing common life circumstances (think military wives or preschool mothers), and those we spend a lot of time with socially. "Outer Heart" friends also reserve a special place in our lives and we love and trust them greatly.

Around the outside border of the heart are the "Heart Potential" friends. These are people you see now and then but don't really know very well—more acquaintances rather than friends. They are "Heart Potential" because while you don't know them intimately now, you like them enough to consider developing a friendship with them at some point. Finally, anyone outside of the hearts or heart potential areas are people you either don't know or don't consider as friends.

Heart Sisters are born from any of the three inner hearts. These are the women who get you, who know what lies inside your heart and love you anyway, and who walk beside you unconditionally. You can reveal your ugly stuff to Heart Sisters and they won't judge—in fact, they're often right there saying, "Me too!" These are the women who will speak truth into your life, who will watch your children when you don't want to take all three of them to your doctor's appointment, and who will encourage you to be the person God created you to be by not letting you off the hook when you misstep because they're afraid of hurting your feelings. Heart Sisters are essential to our mental, physical, and spiritual growth.

The dynamic of the relationship between Jesus and His three "Inner Heart" friends is definitely worth studying. Peter, James, and John were His go-to guys among the twelve disciples. In fact, they were the only disciples to have witnessed some very tender and vulnerable moments during His ministry. These three were present at the raising of Jairus's daughter as well as the only other humans to witness the Transfiguration. The Transfiguration is one of the most intimate moments of Jesus' life, and He wanted only His three Inner Heart friends present to bear witness.

And while it's true that the relationship between these men was often the mentor (Jesus) to the mentee (Peter, James, and John), there were moments in which Jesus revealed authentic vulnerability as well. Besides the Transfiguration, these three men were asked to stand guard while Jesus prayed at Gethsemane. Yes, they pretty much failed this mission since all three fell asleep; however, the point is that Jesus still sought them to "get His back." The fact that they didn't really have His back was covered by His grace because Jesus was keenly aware of our flesh limitations.

Even among the three, Peter held a very close spot within Jesus' heart. Early on, Jesus identified him as a leader and promised to make this fisherman and his partner, Andrew, "fishers of men." Originally named Simon, Peter was honored when Jesus gave him his new name, which means "rock." Jesus had big plans for Peter to be rock-solid in his teachings of the early church found in the book of Acts.

Peter was impulsive and passionate, outspoken and bold. He often acted and spoke without thinking—in fact, Jesus was keenly aware of where Peter needed guidance and maturity. Though a close brother to Jesus and a protégé of sorts, he still denied him three times when asked if he knew Jesus. He took his eyes off of Jesus when he walked on the water and sank. He cut off the high priest's servant's ear when Jesus was arrested. He was far from perfect, yet Jesus knew all of this would occur even when he chose him to be a disciple. He offered Peter mercy and grace and was able to look beyond the junk that sometimes surfaced in his soul to see the leadership potential and other positive qualities that led to the expansion of the church after Jesus' death. Peter was one of Jesus' most beloved friends because even when his actions were so unpredictable, Jesus was able to see his heart.

On the other hand, brothers John and James were maybe both a little less outspoken than Peter, but not by much. Nicknamed with his brother the "Sons of Thunder" perhaps because of their fiery tempers, John was also known as the "Apostle of Love" and craved time with Jesus. He adored the church and encouraged its members to get along and love one another. He handled those who were legalistic with love and gentleness but was also firm when he needed to be firm. In addition, he was very trustworthy and brave. John had the courage to go to the foot of the cross during Jesus' crucifixion when the other disciples were still in hiding, and he was entrusted to stand with Jesus' mother, Mary, during the last moments of her son's life. He was also known to be a strong intercessor and he certainly knew his Scriptures.

Much less is known about his brother James, likely because his life was cut short—he was the first to die as a martyr of

Christianity. However, it is thought that he was courageous (obviously) and particularly forgiving. It is also believed he did not succumb to jealousy as he often lived in the shadow of his more popular brother, John.

While Peter, John, and James make up the Inner Heart friends of Jesus, there are other relationships Jesus held dear as well. Bartholomew was considered to be honest and straightforward. Martha showed Jesus immense hospitality while her sister Mary was loyal and unwavering. He had a diverse array of friends who fulfilled different roles within his own life.

The last friendship relationship we'll discuss deviates from Jesus' relationships and is one of my favorites—the friendship between Elizabeth and Mary. As we read in the first chapter of Luke, Gabriel visits Mary and informs her she has been chosen by God to give birth to the Christ child. Despite the fact she is a virgin, Mary accepts this and days later embarks upon a journey to visit her cousin, Elizabeth. Now, let's face it—don't you think your mind would be spinning a bit if you were Mary? She was believed to have been about fourteen years old when this all occurred, and although I understand that a fourteen-year-old living in biblical times was quite different from a fourteen-year-old now, we can still conclude that Mary likely needed a little bit of encouragement.

The encouragement she didn't even know she needed was offered by Elizabeth, who strongly proclaimed,

> You're so blessed among women,
>   and the babe in your womb, also blessed!
> And why am I so blessed that
>   the mother of my Lord visits me?

The moment the sound of your
  greeting entered my ears,
The babe in my womb
  skipped like a lamb for sheer joy.
Blessed woman, who believed what God said,
  believed every word would come true! (Luke
1:39-45 THE MESSAGE)

Perhaps this was just what Mary needed to hear because it then led her to praise the Lord with the Magnificat, which is one of her most revered moments in scripture. Never underestimate the power of encouragement. Heart Sisters encourage, not discourage.

So based upon the friends of Jesus, what kind of friends should we seek? If an iron sharpens iron (Proverbs 27:17), the Super Seven Sisters are your girls. While having a group of Super Seven Sisters is a goal we can work toward, it should also be stated there are no hard-and-fast rules here. Maybe your Martha friend is also your Mary friend. The quality of our friendships is more important than the quantity of friends we have. On the other hand, while you may not have seven close friends, it's also less than ideal to have just one girlfriend because that one girlfriend cannot be your everything. This can put too much pressure on her shoulders, and your friendship may suffer.

It's also possible to have a whole host of friends but none that walk deeply with your heart. I've been in this situation before, and it's a lonely place to be. Though you may often be surrounded by people, having too many "surface" friendships will cause your heart to feel unheard, increase your desire to just be known, and make you feel as if something is missing in your relationships—you just might not know what that something is. Perhaps author Kim Culbertson said it best in her book *The Liberation of Max McTrue*, "People think being alone makes you lonely, but I don't think that's true. Being surrounded by the wrong people is the loneliest thing in the world."[1]

The Super Seven Sisters are:

1. **Rahab:** This woman is bold and will speak for you when you can't. She's courageous and will lovingly speak truth if you aren't living your life for God. Rahab friends are willing to be honest while keeping your best interest a top priority.

2. **Mary:** Your Mary friend is very trustworthy and is one of your prayer warriors. Even if you don't communicate with her regularly, you know when push comes to shove, she's going to be there for you and defend you to the end.

3. **Deborah:** Deborah friends are strong leaders and have been gifted with wisdom. When a crisis strikes, she will remain level-headed and calm. She's also your girl to run to for wise counsel.

4. **Naomi:** These friends are older than you and serve as a spiritual mentor.

5. **Ruth:** These friends are loyal and unwavering. She's in your court no matter what, and pity the fool who dares to cross you! She sticks by you in all circumstances—always.

6. **Bathsheba:** Bathsheba sisters have been through some hard stuff and lived to tell about it. They'll walk through adversity with you and help you remember this isn't the end of your story because God will use it for His glory. A Bathsheba friend is a tough one with just the right balance of truth and grace, and she's a restorer of hope that inspires you to keep going one day at a time.

7. **Elizabeth:** Your Elizabeth friend possesses the gift of encouragement. She builds you up when you need a pep talk, and she will always point you to the truth.

In the end, the Super Seven Sisters are your "people," the ones you want to have with you when you walk through the parts of life that just plain stink and the ones you want to have with you when life is all good. During Jesus' life, there were five major milestones: His baptism, transfiguration, crucifixion, resurrection, and ascension. If we examine all of these milestones, we see various friends of His heart were present for each. John the Baptist baptized Him. Peter, James, and John were present at the transfiguration. John, Mary Magdalene, Mary (mother of Jesus), and a few of His female followers witnessed the crucifixion. Mary Magdalene also discovered Jesus' empty tomb (along with some unidentified followers of Jesus), which proved His resurrection. Shortly thereafter, Jesus visited the disciples, who, forty days later, were the only people present to witness His ascension to heaven. Jesus surrounded Himself with those He loved during the intimate moments of His life. Your Heart Sisters are the women you want to be around during your *own* major milestones. They will hold you up when you're falling but will also rejoice with you when there's rejoicing to be done.

While the Super Seven Sisters focus primarily on an individual personality type, we should also discuss the different groups of friends we may encounter in our lives. The top five groups of friends most women have in their lives are online friends, real-life friends, "Narrow Path" friends, mentor/mentee friends, and ministry friends. Again, you may not have friends in each of these categories, and you might have a friend who fits in each of these categories!

I've been in the blog world now for a little over three years. As is the case with many other bloggers, I've met some of my Heart Sisters online through the blogosphere. They are beautiful people—gone are the days in which it was considered a little weird to meet someone online. These friends and I "get" each other pretty easily because we are serving in the same ministry (and they're also my ministry friends, whom we'll discuss soon). In addition to fellow bloggers, I have met some dear friends through a few online groups I lead as well.

However, I must say that while the popularity of online communities continues to grow, we also need to recognize that face-to-face relationships can be compromised if we get too embedded in the online world. While we can certainly have wonderful online friendships, it's critical to also possess in-real-life friends because they're the ones who will be able to deliver dinner after you've had surgery. They're the ones who can help you watch your children so you can go to the store—alone. They're the ones who will be able to be physically available to sit with you while you cry and laugh with you when you just need to laugh. When we choose to have only online friends and forego those real-life relationships, we are short changing ourselves, sisters. We do real life with real life friends.

Since we're on the subject of in-real-life friends, let's talk about cliques. There seems to be a negative connotation to this term, and when used in the way in which it is likely intended, I understand why this is so. However, I've thought much about this as of late because God has blessed me with a group of true Heart Sisters that have organically formed into a group of very close-knit friends. They are my sisters in every sense of the word and, as I said at the opening of this book, I've always desired a

Tight-knit friends have tight-knit faith.

sister! It's truly a huge blessing, and yet it's been quite a road to get to this point. If you looked at us from the outside, you might think we were a clique; however, there's actually a difference between a clique and a tight-knit group of friends.

Cliques are based upon exclusivity and the leaving out of others. They imply that certain criteria exist for another to gain acceptance into the clique as well as a "testing" period for a new member to gain entry. In addition, members of a clique will often gossip about one another and oftentimes secretly discourage each other because of underlying issues of jealousy. Cliques are self-centered and self-serving.

On the other hand, a tight-knit group of friends naturally tends to spend a lot of time together because they love each other and are committed to spurring one another on. They actively seek prayer requests from each other and inquire about updates on those prayer requests. They laugh together and know one another's family well. They enhance the others' lives through their support, love, and commitment. Each member of this tight-knit group of friends is confident they are not being spoken of negatively among themselves, and they subscribe to a biblical way of living through handling conflict in a way that honors Christ. Close friends choose relationship every time—even if it means they won't necessarily be justified or win the war of being "right." They are simply one another's safe haven. Tight-knit friends have tight-knit faith.

One of the differences between a clique and a tight-knit group of friends is how they welcome others. If someone were to approach a specific group of friends, how would she be received? Would she be ignored? Made to feel like she's not enough? If so, this group of friends is likely a clique. However, if you are welcomed and valued for who you are when you approach this group of friends and are immediately included in conversation, then you are likely encountering a tight-knit group of friends. If they are supportive of each other and don't dwell on the negative, they're tight-knit friends. If they incessantly put down their significant others, focus on material items, and speak ill of one another, they're a clique. It's important to discern the difference between cliques and tight-knit groups of friends because incorrectly labeling a group of women as a clique might deprive you of some very dear Heart Sisters!

Another kind of friend is a "Narrow Path" friend. Narrow Path friends help us stay on the path that leads to God and encourage us to stay obedient to Him in our everyday lives. While some may call this type of relationship "accountability partners" there's just something about the word *accountability* that sounds so formal and too "by-the-rules" to me. My Narrow Path friend (who is also an Inner Heart friend) is one of my most committed prayer warriors. She also offers advice from a biblical perspective when my marriage hits a rough patch or I am challenged by my children or anything else that makes me want to react in the flesh rather than in the Spirit. She is a safe person who intimately knows my heart, and she sharpens me big-time!

I'm also a huge believer in mentoring friends and being mentored ourselves. I've always been drawn to Titus 2:3 in which the older women are instructed to teach the younger women to do good. While the person you are mentoring might be older in chronological years than you, she might be younger than you in her walk with God. Similarly, your own personal mentor might be younger than you in years but older in her relationship with the Lord! This being said, I have found real value in meeting with a mentor who is both chronologically and spiritually older than me. Recognizing my need for someone like this in my life, I prayed fervently for God to reveal a woman who loved Him and would be willing to serve as my mentor. We are called to reach up to the wiser and down to the ones reaching up to us. Of course, we're reaching down figuratively and not condescendingly!

An example of this in the Bible can be seen between Jesus and Peter. Peter reached up to Jesus because he was being trained to be a leader of the disciples and the church body in general. He reached down to the rest of the disciples and other followers of Jesus. But did you notice how Peter still reached down even though he wasn't perfect or the model Christ-follower? You don't have to arrive as a Christian to thrive as a mentor.

Finally, another group of friends we may have is ministry friends. These are the peers who serve with you in a common ministry. Your ministry friends can also be your online friends, real-life friends, and your mentor/mentee friends. They can offer support when you feel criticized or help you spread the word when you need to raise a bit of awareness about what you're doing. They're on your team and believe in your ministry. They're a wealth of information as you begin the process of ministry whether it's by beginning a new one or joining the leadership team of one that already exists. You're in it together and you share a common goal—to glorify God and lead others to Him.

My prayer for you right now is that you aren't sitting there thinking, *Well, Natalie, all of this is great, but where on earth do I find these Super Seven Sisters and groups of friends?* I started completely from scratch eight years ago. A blank slate. It took a whole lot of courage and made me reach past my comfort zone. If you tend to be introverted by nature, I recognize how difficult it can be to put yourself out there. Really, I get it. I'm personally not an introvert but rather an ambivert—I'm both. So in some respects, I get where you're coming from, introverts.

Cultivating Heart Sister relationships can take time. Be patient with the process—the most important thing is to just show up and stay in the game.

However, we don't ever grow if we stay where it's easy and comfortable, do we? When I recognized my need for girlfriends, I knew they weren't going to just show up on my front doorstep. I had to choose to step outside of my safe haven and do a few things that scared me. I joined a Mothers of Preschoolers (MOPS) group where I didn't know anyone. I volunteered to help with their events so I could get to know the members better. I enrolled in our church's Bible study. I smiled and said hello when I dropped my children off at preschool and picked them up. I hosted playdates. I share this not so you will say, "Good for you!" but rather so you'll grasp the hope that is there—if I can do it, so can you!

I want to end this chapter with a bit of encouragement. Cultivating Heart Sister relationships can take time. Be patient with the process—the most important thing is to just show up and stay in the game. Be present in the lives of your budding friendships. Offer support and encouragement. Pray for her. In other words, be a friend. Because while it is often a cliché, the old adage of "you have to be a friend to get a friend" is actually quite true.

DISCUSSION QUESTIONS

1. Can you identify Inner Heart, Middle Heart, and Outer Heart friends? Why do you think they're important?

2. Which type of Super Seven Sister do you think you might be? Why? What type of Super Seven Sister are some of your friends?

3. Do you have a mentor? If so, how has she influenced your life? If you didn't, is this something you might want to pray about finding?

4. Is there someone YOU might be able to mentor?

5. Do you have online friends? If so, how are they different from real-life friends?

CHAPTER FOUR

CLASH OF THE TITANS
Muddling Through Conflict

*The most beautiful discovery true friends make is that
they can grow separately without growing apart.*
Elisabeth Foley

L et's take a moment to come to grips with something
here. We are all, every single one of us, disabled by a
tricky little ailment called "the flesh." When I say tricky,
I mean it's deception at its finest—it shields us from complete
surrender and trust in God, and it makes us think the world is
all about us. It can also disguise our need for recognition and
fame through works rather than faith, and it can force us to
give little grace to others because how dare they, even though
we've done the same and seem to have forgotten the grace
that was extended to us? Worst of all, that pesky flesh disease is
the main culprit behind our inability to remove the log from our
own eye.

The apples were sweet. The serpent was convincing. Adam
and Eve were weak when faced with temptation. Our flesh disability entered the world, and we've been afflicted ever since.

Yet here we are, living each day with the consequences of the generational sin that began with the red, juicy apple and the serpent's suggestion of doubt that offered an alternate choice of power in oneself and not the God above. "Did God *really* say, 'You must not eat from any tree in the garden'?" (Genesis 3:1, emphasis mine). Eve fell for it, and Adam didn't stop her.

This isn't how God planned it to be. He planned for us all to live long and prosper in that beautiful garden with no weeds and easy childbirth (which, for all you mothers out there, might increase your frustration just a bit). He meant for us to be in such close communion with Him and feel His presence so acutely we would absolutely know without a shadow of a doubt He is real and present. As a result of this deeper, uncomplicated relationship with Him, relational strife with others simply wouldn't exist because we would resemble Him completely. He also planned for the snake to walk upright, for crying out loud.

All of God's plan was changed with one simple bite.

Sadly, it's our nature to give in to this disability, but let's not forget there's always hope. Thankfully, our God doesn't leave us high and dry. Remember the promise from Hebrews 13:5: "Never will I leave you; never will I forsake you."

God being God, He seemed to have had this all figured out when His gift of freewill went awry because He ultimately provided us all with a guidebook that makes it as clear as day as to how we are to live. On that note, may I digress a moment and tell you how many self-help books I have purchased when the best one resided right in my home all along? I never claimed to be a quick learner! The Bible has it all, sisters—stories of passionate romance, relational conflicts galore, and more power struggles than we can even imagine. God's truth changes our diagnosis. We are flesh-disabled, but Jesus-enabled.

Since each of us suffers from this disability of the flesh, it's an inevitable fact there will be a conflict at some point in each of our close relationships. It's not an "if" but a

God's truth changes our diagnosis. We are flesh-disabled, but Jesus-enabled.

"when"—it *will* happen. John 16:33 says, "In this world you *will* have trouble" (but blessedly goes on to encourage us to not lose heart because Jesus has overtaken the world. Whew). The trouble to which Jesus is referring most often occurs in our personal relationships. It doesn't say maybe it will happen. He says it *will* indeed happen, whether we like it or not.

It's guaranteed tough times and conflict with others will be a part of our existence on this side of heaven. There's really no way around it. If we are going to love our neighbors as ourselves, we have to interact with others. If we are interacting with others, we will indeed be faced with conflict at some point.

And again, God being God, He's known this all along. He knew we would have trouble with relationships. Therefore, He knew He would need to give us some guidelines. God also knew the resulting relationships that weathered the storm would reward those willing to do the tough work with a closeness that could only come through trial. Trust is developed because when we discover that a friend values our friendship and he or she is willing to walk through the muck to save it, we see what God meant when He said a brother (or a sister) is born for adversity (Proverbs 17:17). Among the women who are my true Heart Sisters, three of them became sisters of the heart after we walked through conflict that could have derailed our friendship and left us without the benefit of having sisterhood in our lives. I shudder at the thought.

Three years ago, I remember feeling gripped with sadness as I sat on the phone with my dear Heart Sister, Melinda. We were both leaders in the same women's ministry and had been talking about an issue we weren't seeing in the same light (hysterically enough, I can't even recall the issue today—that's how pressing it was!). The conversation suddenly succumbed to both of our frustrations, and we said things we should not have said. We hung up the phone but we both knew the conflict was unresolved. When conflict is unresolved and I feel that someone is upset with me, I'm consumed. Melinda is the same way.

After I'd had a few moments to cool off, I called her. I could tell she had been crying, so I said, "I'm bringing coffee. I'll stop at Starbucks and be over!" We proceeded to have a healthy discussion over lattes and apologized for the words we had said in anger. Melinda and I entered into a deeper level of friendship because we both came to the table with humble hearts and we valued our relationship more than being right or getting our own way. Just last month, we came to another bump in the road, and guess what? We knew we could speak to one another candidly about what was happening in our hearts because we had done it in the past. Choosing relationship over being right allows us to win the battle and the war. Melinda is one of my very dearest Heart Sisters, and we've gotten there by walking through conflict in a way that honors God.

I would like to say all of the conflicts I've ever experienced with women ended so beautifully, but alas, that is so very much not the case. Eight years ago when I was living in Indianapolis,

I had a dear friend who was a big part of my daily life. Our children were the same ages, attended the same school, and we had playdates where the kids played and the moms talked. We were very close and our children were as well.

But something happened. She didn't agree with a decision I made in the ministry I was leading at the time, and I didn't agree with her. As in my conflict with Melinda, we had a few tense moments. However, unlike my conflict with Melinda, my attempts to discuss what had happened and move toward reconciliation were met with rejection. Each time I asked to meet with her, she said she preferred to not ever talk about it and move on in our friendship—but I can't do that because if I can't talk through a conflict in any of my close relationships, I feel like trust has been compromised. Conflict *will* happen when we are in relationship with other people. If I feel like I can't talk it through, then trust will chisel away and the friendship will likely not survive.

So what's a girl to do when stuff comes up and trouble starts to brew? Let's take a look at how to handle conflict or address someone when something just feels different in the relationship by meeting our good friend P.E.G.

1. PRAY

> If any of you lacks wisdom, you should ask God, who gives generously to all without finding fault, and it will be given to you. But when you ask, you must believe and not doubt, because the one who doubts is like a wave of the sea, blown and tossed by the wind.
>
> James 1:5-6

I'm guilty of a lot of things, but one in particular is my immediate desire to jump on the phone with a trusted friend when a relational conflict arises. I justify this by telling myself I'm seeking wise counsel, but I've skipped a step. God is the ultimate dispenser of wise counsel. I first need to pray and ask Him to reveal my own sin. I need help in removing the log from my own eye and to be given the wisdom I need to handle conflict in a manner that glorifies Him. In a different translation of the above passage, he tells us, "If any of you lacks wisdom, let him ask God, who gives generously to all without reproach, and it will be given him. But let him ask in faith, with no doubting, for the one who doubts is like a wave of the sea that is driven and tossed by the wind" (ESV). Notice it doesn't say this wisdom *might* be given to you—it says it *will* be given to you if you believe in God and don't doubt who He is. When we're stuck and we can't budge, the Holy Spirit will provide the nudge.

2. EXAMINE

> *Why do you look at the speck of sawdust in your brother's eye and pay no attention to the plank in your own eye? How can you say to your brother, "Let me take the speck out of your eye," when all the time there is a plank in your own eye? You hypocrite, first take the plank out of your own eye, and then you will see clearly to remove the speck from your brother's eye.*
>
> Matthew 7:3-5

Good thing there's no mincing of words here, right? At times that log in my own eye has been so big, I've had to call in a construction crew to get it out. No, it's not fun, sisters, but remember— the fruit that's produced is worth the effort. Ask yourself the following questions:

A. What's my role in this? Like it or not, the most innocent can still have a role. Not long ago, a friend of mine was hurt by something I did. The truth of the matter is, it had been an emotional twenty-four hours for me and I was running on two hours of sleep. Through prayer the following morning (in the shower of all places!) it became evident to me that I needed to go to her and apologize for what I did and explain that it wasn't intended to hurt her. While it wasn't received in the manner I had hoped it would be, that's OK because it's about obedience to Him and not necessarily about things you can't control—like how someone will respond to you. When we follow through in obedience, we do our part before the Lord. God has His own thing going on with the other person. It's important to remember in these situations that you can't change someone—only the Holy Spirit has the power to do that.

B. Am I hurt because of my own insecurity? So often I have reacted to others negatively because I felt guilty of something I've failed to do, and deep down, I knew I was wrong. Is there a trigger from my own brokenness that this friend has unknowingly set off? Is this more of a "me" thing than a "her" thing?

C. Am I expecting too much? Are my standards too high? Let me just tell you . . . This is one boat I've rowed again and again. Here's the deal: there's a God-shaped hole in all of us and so very often, we women expect it to be filled by our sideways relationships rather than our vertical relationship with Him. The reason why so many people flit from relationship to relationship is there's not a person alive that can fill that God-shaped hole—only God can. If you are expecting too much out of your friend, she will eventually feel that pressure and start to back off—and in case you're wondering, your husband or significant other will too.

This is why getting right with God is a must if you desire healthy relationships. Are you expecting her to make you her number one priority—even over God, and her family? Are you making her feel guilty if she chooses to stay home and watch TV because she just needs a little "down time" instead of going out with you? Are you expecting hour-long chat sessions when she is in an extremely busy season of work? Our own emotional baggage should not be dictating the expectations and overall tone of our friendships because there's not a person alive who can be our everything. Only God has the ability to be our everything.

D. Will I be able to spend time with her without thinking of this hurt? If you feel as if failure to address this hurt will force you to overreact to every little flaw in your friend and your guard is always up when you're with her, then it probably needs to be discussed.

E. Can I trust this person? Will I be able to be vulnerable with her? If you're unwilling to go deep, it's surface friendships you'll reap. If you won't allow a friend past your front porch without inviting her into your living room or, even better, your bathroom, you're simply just going to have a surface friendship. It should also be stated that not all friendships will be deep friendships. Surface friendships are fine in some cases; however, if all of your friendships are surface friendships, you're robbing yourself of the long list of benefits to having a Heart Sister. On another note, if the woman you are in conflict with is someone you've let into your living room in the past, the elephant in the room likely needs to be addressed.

3. Go

Therefore, if you are offering your gift at the altar and there remember that your brother or sister has something against you, leave your gift there in front of the altar. First go and be reconciled to them; then come and offer your gift.

Matthew 5:23-24

This Matthew verse tells us to lay down any gift of worship we are bringing to His altar if we have a brother or sister who might be disgruntled with us or if there is relational discord that hasn't properly been concluded. Simply GO. Not always what I want to do, if I may be completely candid with you, but like it or not, Jesus calls us to go. He calls us to take the initiative, even if we are innocent, to begin the healing and reconciliation process because He always desires for us to choose relationship. No exceptions.

And while we're on this topic, isn't this precisely what Jesus did for us? Sin entered the world and broke our relationship with God. Jesus was without fault—He didn't eat the apple. Yet God told Him to go—*go* take the initiative to restore relationship even though you are completely innocent; *go* and choose relationship at all costs; *go* and do all you can to live in peace among everyone. He makes us friends with God because He went when He was told to *go*. Jesus was innocent but God told Him to finish it, so He did.

Recently, while preparing to speak to a group about female relationships, I realized that the writing and preparation I was doing was indeed an act of worship. I am passionate about encouraging women to live in sisterhood with one another, and my desire is for it to be done in a way that glorifies God through the power of love and grace. However, I realized there was an unresolved conflict between another friend and me that still didn't have complete closure. I didn't want to go, but can I tell you how disastrous the results are when I fail to listen to the still, small voice that is nudging me *to* go? I didn't have a choice because who am I to speak and write on this topic but then not do what God says we are to do?

I need to also tell you how many times I have failed to go in the past: I have about twenty other miserable attempts to go along with my one success. But go I did, and I attempted to reconcile the relationship. The results were not what I desired; however, I learned that conflict resolution won't always be tied up with a big red bow at the end (more on this in the next chapter). That particular friend chose not to work through the hard stuff, but at least I know I did all I could do to choose relationship instead of strife. I could place the gift back on the altar.

Perhaps one of the greatest illustrations from the Bible of one who felt the urge to go back to someone after a conflict is Hagar. Sarai began to grow a little impatient with her barren womb and strongly suggested that Abram father a child with her maidservant, Hagar. Abram obliged and an impregnated Hagar began to resent her mistress for forcing her into such a precarious situation. Sarai soon realized she had made a mistake as well and began to treat Hagar unkindly. Not knowing what else to do, Hagar fled.

While Hagar was resting at a well, an angel from the Lord spoke to her and urged her to go back to her mistress and "submit to her." As a reward, the angel reassured Hagar that God would give her too many descendants to count and honor her with a son. This is the point in which she utters one of my favorite sentences of the Bible: "You are the God who sees me," she says (Genesis 16:13). The fact that Sarai and she never became bosom buddies after their conflict is not the point but rather Hagar's obedience to the Lord to go in humility when she was called to do so.

Did you notice how Hagar's first reaction was to flee the scene? It's our natural inclination to get out of uncomfortable situations as quickly as possible because truthfully, it's easier to simply not have to deal with it, isn't it? I won't argue with that particular point—sometimes, it is indeed easier to walk away from a relationship that's gotten difficult. But here's the thing: eventually, there will be some kind of conflict in every single one of our deeper relationships. The only way to ensure this *won't* happen is to keep your relationships at a surface level. If you only have "front porch friends," friends who just see what's on the outside and are never invited into your living room, you won't have to risk the threat of relational conflict—but you'll be a very lonely woman.

When we have the courage to walk through conflict with a friend, as Hagar did with Sarai and my friend did with me, we are also rewarded. We're rewarded with a deeper level of friendship. We are rewarded with a friend who has just gotten to know us that much more. We are rewarded with a friend who has expressed the level of her safety to you through her willingness to listen to your heart with humility and grace. It's true many choose to follow their initial reaction to flee when relationships get difficult; yet in doing so, they miss the fruit of reconciliation. It's OK for friends to disagree, but a true Heart Sister is one who won't flee. She'll stick it out and talk it out.

I wish I could tell you every time I've had a conflict with a friend it's had a happy ending but sadly, I can't. While my friendship with Melinda grew deeper because we were able to have humble hearts and commit to our relationship rather than arguing about which of us was right, I've had a few friendships where the opposite was true. Although God desires reconciliation for all of His followers, the reality is that it doesn't always happen. It takes one to forgive but two to reconcile. Melinda and I both desired reconciliation because we are true Heart Sisters and not reconciling was simply not an option; it took two of us to reconcile and we did. We will talk more about forgiveness in the next chapter, but you can choose to forgive without being asked for forgiveness, and you can forgive yourself even if you haven't been forgiven—so it only takes one to forgive: you.

Let's say we've prayed and examined and we're feeling the unmistakable nudge to "go," which is a good thing considering what we've discussed thus far. Have you ever gotten a feeling about something you just can't shake? Ever think something along the lines of *I'm really feeling like I should* _____? Often it is the Holy Spirit prompting you to do what God desires for you. In 2011, I innocently felt God nudging me to choose *obedience* as my word for the year. Let me just tell you—if you ever feel nudged to choose this word as your focus for the year, hold on to your hat, sisters. You'll be amazed at what He has for you.

I was unaware of the evil twins that are a part of disobedience—their names are pride and lack of humility. Pride and lack of humility will work in tandem to derail your plans of obedience because, well, it can be tough to let go of our pride and even tougher to face our mistakes in humility. But you want to know what's worse? When we try to brush off God's requests because what He's asking us to do makes us squirm a bit. I don't know about you, but I've never grown in my walk with Him without some kind of discomfort.

Pride is a sneaky little trait that grips everyone with flesh at some point. In the past, when I thought of those who were prideful, I envisioned individuals who were insecure and therefore needed to boast about their goodness—they were "proud" of everything from their job performance to their child's academic success to their physical attributes to the amount in their bank account. It wasn't until I began to struggle with some of my own pride issues that I recognized them for what they were. I didn't like to leave my children if I went on a much-needed vacation with my husband because, ultimately, I didn't believe anyone else could take care of them the way I could. I didn't want to accept help because I was supposed to be the one that always helped others and not the other way around.

In conjunction with lack of humility, pride has the power to derail every single relationship it digs its deep roots into. Pride blocks vulnerability, and vulnerability is the gatekeeper of authentic relationships. I believe every negative emotion can be traced back to fear, and pride is no exception. In our house, as well as in many other homes, the kitchen tends to be where everyone gathers. It's also where I produce nourishment for my family. If vulnerability is the door in which authentic relationship enters, our humble heart is the kitchen that cooks the relationship and provides the nourishment it needs to grow.

Pride can both look and sound like the following in a female friendship:

- "No, I don't need any help. I've got it all under control."

- "I'm not in the wrong here so I'm not going to attempt to repair this relationship. I'll wait for her since she's in the wrong. Until then, I just won't talk to her."

- "I can't forgive her because she hasn't asked me for forgiveness."

- "No, I've never struggled with_____."

- "No, I won't meet with you to discuss our conflict. Our relationship has just sailed its course and I've moved on."

Before we go on to discuss lack of humility, let's first look at what humility really is (as this once confused me). Being humble doesn't only mean you don't toot your own horn. It means you accept you will mess up from time to time and might need to apologize for it to boot. It means going to someone in a nonaccusatory manner to seek understanding without assuming you have done nothing wrong and being willing to own your part and move toward reconciliation. Here's what lack of humility looks like and sounds like in a female friendship:

- "What are you so uptight about?"

- "I know I didn't do anything wrong, so I know you aren't mad at me, but what's bothering you?"

- "OK" or any other generic phrase that neither accepts an apology nor admits any wrongdoing on her own part after someone approaches the responder with a humble apology for her role in a conflict. This is also a pride issue—see how pride and lack of humility are such good coworkers?

- Accepting an apology but refusing to examine your own role in the conflict regardless of "who did more" to hurt the other.

During the two years I was knee-deep in women's ministry, I noticed one key factor that determined if a friendship would last: the presence of humility. Friends who were able to go to

Once we humble ourselves to the Lord, humbling ourselves to others becomes a bit easier. Humility is the key that unlocks hearts.

one another with humble hearts by owning their part, seeking to reconcile, and choosing relationship instead of strife were the ones who actually entered a deeper level of intimacy with one another and became Heart Sisters. The relationships that disintegrated were almost always due to a complete lack of humility either on both sides or just one. Remember when I said in the introduction that much of what we discuss here will also apply to other relationships? Here's a nugget that reaches across all divides: humility is the foundation to all safe and healthy relationships. John 3:30 says, "He must increase, but I must decrease." However, we can't allow Him to increase without humbling ourselves. Once we humble ourselves to the Lord, humbling ourselves to others becomes a bit easier. Humility is the key that unlocks hearts.

So, let's say you have a friend you're feeling called to go to in order to ensure all is well between the two of you, but you're not exactly sure *how* to go to her. Perhaps the thought of addressing conflict makes you break out in a cold sweat and you just want to brush it under the rug and not deal with it because living with the festering hurt seems easier—though ultimately, it's not. How do we handle this in a way that is pleasing and glorifying to God?

Entering into conflict can be tenuous because the enemy attacks relationship more than anything else and would like nothing more than to see Jesus' followers living in strife with one another because, really, who would want to be a part of *that*? No pressure, of course, but we can begin to see the kingdom impact of failed relationships—if His followers are biting, devouring, and destroying one another (Galatians 5:15), doesn't this send a very confusing message to those who either don't believe or are new believers? Not to mention living this way would cause a huge amount of undue stress, model unhealthy relational behavior and, most important, be in disobedience since we are told to "as far as it depends on you, live at peace with everyone" (Romans 12:18).

If we've determined that indeed we need to discuss an issue with a friend, our first step is to go to her regardless of who is to blame—a private discussion between only the parties involved.

But what happens when there hasn't been a particular conflict with a friend but something is just different in the relationship? Perhaps she has pulled away from you by suddenly being unavailable for coffee or playdates with the kids and you almost always receive her voicemail without a return call. Again, we are called to go although we might not want to do so! Can we all just vow to memorize the following sentence and promise to use it when we think things are off in any of our female relationships?

"Have I hurt or offended you in any way?"

If the answer is no, then you've shown her you value your friendship enough to check in and be sure you haven't inadvertently hurt her. If the answer is yes, then it's your job to listen with a humble heart—without interruptions and without formulating your response while she's speaking. Instead, just listen. Hear what she has to say and apologize for your role. Own it so you can choose relationship and move toward reconciliation.

However, it's true God has created us all to be different from one another. If you are one that needs more time to think, you can simply state, "I need more time to think about this, but I apologize if I've hurt you in any way." Stating that we are sorry to have hurt someone doesn't admit guilt—it simply means that something we said or did hurt the person and we are simply sorry for that hurt alone. For example, if you have lovingly rebuked someone who was obviously choosing to succumb to sin, apologizing for speaking to her would not be something you would want to do; however, if she comes to you and says she was hurt by your words, you can apologize for the hurt she felt but not necessarily for the words you are expected as a Heart Sister to speak. (This is kind of like apologizing to a child who fell down and skinned his knee. We say we are sorry that this has happened and acknowledge his hurt even though it wasn't our fault he fell down.) In fact, I strongly suggest devising a conflict plan with close friends and groups of women who serve or work together so everyone is on the same page. There is a "Heart Sisters Agreement" on my blog if you are interested in discussing this further (www.nataliesnapp.com).

Mark Twain once said, "A true friend stabs you in the front." In the same vein, my friend Kiersten talks about friends having a "light-switch privilege" in which you aren't judging their behavior; you just simply want to turn the light on for them. Healthy conflict resolution is a way both parties can turn the light on for each other, and as a result, have a more illuminated relationship that squelches the darkness. Heart Sisters turn on the lights and stab you in the front so the darkness is defeated.

DISCUSSION QUESTIONS

1. Have you ever walked through a conflict with a friend that didn't go so well? What would you do differently if you could?

2. Why do you think humility is so important when talking to a friend about a conflict?

3. Do you have a conflict plan with any of your friends? If so, what have you agreed to do when conflict arises? If not, what are you thoughts on discussing this with your friends?

4. How do you react to conflict? Do you try to avoid it and "sweep everything under the rug"? Do you take responsibility for offenses even when you aren't guilty so there can be peace? Do you speak before you think? Reflect on this for a moment and ask the Lord to reveal what He wants you to do when conflict arises.

5. Has pride ever negatively impacted any of your personal relationships?

CHAPTER FIVE

THE FORGIVENESS BUSINESS

To be Christian is to forgive the inexcusable because God has forgiven the inexcusable in you.

C. S. Lewis in *The Weight of Glory*

Let's start this chapter with the truth about forgiveness: it's just plain difficult sometimes, isn't it? Forgiveness is the number one stumbling block most Christians face because it's simply not in our nature to love someone who has hurt or offended us. Our flesh cries out for us to get even when we are at odds with someone else. We are encouraged to settle the score because we live in a society that believes that "an eye for an eye" is still a justifiable reaction when someone hurts us, even though that was abolished with the Law of Moses. We feel rejected, so we rebel because we're in self-preservation mode and we must protect ourselves at all costs, right?

Except, no. We have to learn to truly humble ourselves to the Lord, which in turn teaches us to humble ourselves to others. Having humility means we care less about getting even and being right and more about choosing relationship above all else.

Conflict is inevitable—it's what we do *after* the conflict that matters most. Not to mention oftentimes, others are watching to see how we handle this bump in the road. If anyone else knows about the conflict you've experienced, you have an opportunity to shine the light of Jesus through to them as well as to your offender.

Perhaps you're wondering why on earth you should forgive anyway. I get this—really, I do. I've had to do a lot of forgiveness work in my lifetime, and I've had to be forgiven myself on many occasions. Maybe you've experienced harm at the hand of someone else. Maybe someone said something that hurt your feelings. Maybe you feel rejected because you perceive that someone has chosen someone else over you. Regardless, offenses are not weighted. We are called to forgive every hurt, from the most tragic to the slightest, because they all have the same power over our souls if we leave them alone to fester. Forgiveness is critical because:

1. **If you forgive those who sin against you, your heavenly Father will forgive you. But if you refuse to forgive others, your Father will not forgive your sins (Matthew 6:14-15 NLT):** I guess there's no other way to interpret this, is there? Jesus didn't mince words on this one. Early on in my experience of serving in women's ministry, I would often, with good intentions, reassure others that "there's nothing God won't forgive of you." Yet, I was wrong. He can forgive you of adultery. He'll forgive you if you choose to have an abortion or if you divorce your spouse. He will forgive you of abuse suffered from your own hand. But He won't forgive you if you have withheld forgiveness from someone else or yourself. Since we have been forgiven of so much at the price of His Son, God expects us to do the same.

This is illustrated best in the parable of the unforgiving debtor in Matthew 18:21-35. It begins when Peter, ever the one who wanted to know specifics, goes to Jesus and asks "Lord, how often shall I forgive someone who sins against me? Seven times?" Peter wanted to blow Jesus away with the magnitude of his grace-giving ability because he was expecting Jesus to confirm that three times was sufficient since this is what the rabbis taught during biblical times. Seven would illustrate the mercy of Peter's heart perfectly.

That's not what Jesus was thinking. "No, not seven times," Jesus replied, "but seven times seventy!" (Matthew 18:22 NLT). However, what He really meant was there is no limit to the amount of times we should forgive a truly repentant heart. Jesus was using a figure of speech to illustrate that the need for our forgiveness knows no limit.

He then continued to share the parable of the debtor who didn't reap what had been sown to him. Allow me to paraphrase:

There was a king who wanted to settle his accounts with his servants. A man who owed him money was brought to his throne though the man was unable to pay his debt. As a result, the king ordered the man's family to be sold into slavery as well as any possessions the man owned so he could be paid. "Be patient with me, and I will pay it all," the man begged as he fell to his knees (Matthew 18:26 NLT). The king pitied the servant and chose to pardon him, forgiving him of all that was owed.

Moments later, the forgiven servant left the king to find a man who owed *him* money. Unfortunately, he wasn't as gracious as the king because he grabbed the man who owed him and began to choke him while demanding his money. Ironically, the man who owed the servant pleaded for his patience by uttering the same sentence the servant had spoken to the king just minutes before. Yet the servant refused and had the man imprisoned until the debt could be paid.

When the king heard of this injustice, he summoned the servant at once. The king replied, "You evil servant! I forgave you that tremendous debt because you pleaded with me. Shouldn't you have mercy on your fellow servant, just as I had mercy on you?" (Matthew 18:32-33 NLT). He then sent the man to prison to be tortured until he had paid his entire debt. Jesus ends His parable with "That's what my heavenly Father will do to you if you refuse to forgive your brothers and sisters from your heart" (Matthew 18:35 NLT).

When we accept God's forgiveness but do not forgive those who've hurt us, we are no different than the foolish servant. Does this make you squirm a bit? It sure does me! We are to forgive others' sins against us because we have been forgiven of so much ourselves.

Three words caught my attention in the last sentence of the parable: from your heart. God knows when we clench our teeth and say "I forgive you" yet really inside our hearts, we don't. It's true that sometimes action must precede emotion, but in the end, He wants our hearts to catch up. It's soul disaster if they don't, and it's freedom when they do.

2. The enemy uses our inability to forgive for mass destruction. I was raised in a church that didn't talk much about spiritual warfare. But I know the enemy is very real. His job on earth is to steal, kill, and destroy (John 10:10). Satan delights in stealing trust, killing souls, and destroying families.

One of the enemy's sneakiest tactics is to meddle in our thoughts. He loves to take one small nugget of truth and give it enough inertia to propel it into a bold-faced lie. For example, let's say I've had a day where my children are constantly arguing and I catch one of them in a lie. Then the school calls to say another child of mine had trouble with his behavior. The truth is we are having a bad day. Every family has them. Bad moments don't make bad parents.

Yet when I say good night to my family and lie down in my bed, I can pass the point of no return if I allow Satan entry into my thoughts as I'm reviewing the day. Suddenly my family's tough day becomes about me failing as a mother. I'm not doing the best job with raising them, so they're arguing, telling lies, and misbehaving. I beat myself up over imperfect parenting moments and soon become convinced they might be better off being raised by a pack of wolves than a poor excuse of a mother like me.

Do you see how he operates? He doesn't even have to work very hard at this either. He gets the ball rolling then sits back and grins as we disappear into a downward spiral of lies. We make it so easy for Satan to convince us of the truth in the lies, but we make it hard to identify when he's at work. Since he is the great deceiver, it's often much later in the game when we recognize what's really going on.

Besides our own thoughts, the enemy also loves to attack our relationships because he knows that in doing so, he can deteriorate a thing of beauty created by God. We were made to commune with one another, and relationships are a way in which we can love our neighbor as ourselves. If there is a relationship that has the power to further the kingdom of God, albeit a marriage or a covenant friendship, he'll do his best to see it derailed— through conflict and misunderstanding. Again, he bases it all on one small nugget of truth.

It takes far more courage to forgive than it does not to forgive. It can be tempting to slip into the easy way out if we tend to avoid conflict simply because we don't want to make waves because, let's face it, having the courage to address conflict can be difficult. Yet if we don't give God a chance to shine through the cracks in our clay pots, we lose the opportunity

> Resentment and bitterness are the by-products of unforgiveness, and they're like battery acid to the soul—they'll eat you alive.

to glorify what He can do. God doesn't make strife occur in our relationships—sin does that just fine all by itself and sin is not from God. Sin is from Satan. If we choose to wallow in the consequences of relational sin, then we give the upper hand to the enemy. However, if we choose to redeem that sin, then we glorify God by saying yes to healthy relationships instead of strife. In this case, we give God the upper hand. We can either accept Satan's forgiveness plan or God's forgiveness plan. Rest assured, God's plan is better—even when it's hard.

When a conflict has emerged in a friendship and the steps described in the previous chapter were followed, some level of forgiveness is likely going to be required after the conflict has subsided. Perhaps you're the one who needs to be forgiven or maybe you need to forgive. Maybe it's both. Regardless, it's not really for the sake of your offender that you forgive. It's for you.

3. **Resentment and bitterness are the by-products of unforgiveness, and they're like battery acid to the soul—they'll eat you alive.** Hebrews 12:15 says to "look after each other so

that none of you fails to receive the grace of God. Watch out that no poisonous root of bitterness grows up to trouble you, corrupting many." Bitterness can do a large amount of damage in a small amount of time. It creeps in before we realize it has gained entry and perches in our thoughts until we spew it out in a fury of ugliness that reveals to the world what's in our hearts.

One of my favorite writers, Anne Lamott, once said, "Not forgiving is like drinking rat poison and waiting for the rat to die." Nothing could be more accurate! Bitterness poisons our souls and is so sneaky we usually don't even see it coming. Bitterness is an unexpected but invited guest that brings along resentment and anger. Merriam-Webster defines resentment as "a feeling of indignant displeasure or persistent ill will at something regarded as a wrong, insult, or injury." So if we are feeling ill will toward someone who has wronged us, even if we aren't guilty of a single thing, we risk succumbing to the negativity of resentment if we choose not to forgive. Again, forgiveness is not for the other person—it's for you. When we choose to forgive, we tell bitterness and resentment there's no room at the inn—and we don't even offer them a stable.

4. When we choose to forgive, we model the truths of forgiveness to a very unforgiving world. Get even. Settle the score. Hold a grudge. "Why would you even consider talking to her after she said that?" "Doesn't her misfortune make you so happy? She's getting what she deserves." These are concepts and comments I've heard from well-meaning people who carry their own unforgiveness and don't understand the freedom of letting it go. Sadly enough, this is not all that unusual as we live in a world where the above statements are the norm. An "eye for an eye" mentality is oftentimes glamorized in television

shows and the books and magazines we choose to read. Clearly, another case for guarding our hearts!

When we forgive the unthinkable, it's such a foreign concept to the world that the forgiver is often asked to be interviewed and appear in talk shows. It is actually newsworthy to forgive someone of something so heinous in a world that views forgiveness as a weakness. The mother who forgives the drunk driver for killing her child. The father who forgives his daughter's molester. The woman who forgives her rapist. Incomprehensible, right? Yet these people have discovered that to allow their perpetrator to hold them in chains, they become victims not once, but twice. When you forgive, you remove the power from the person who wronged you and give it back to God. An added bonus is that perhaps the seeds of forgiveness will be planted for others as they watch you forgive.

One of my favorite books is by a woman named Rebecca Nichols Alonzo. In her memoir, *The Devil in Pew Number Seven*, she details her traumatic childhood of being the victim of hate crimes at the hand of a neighbor who disliked her father. As a pastor in a small, Southern town, her father was disliked so fiercely by this man that the man would place dynamite around their yard during the night while they slept. Rebecca and her family were often awakened during the night to the shaking of their walls, shattering glass, and at times, bullets being shot through their windows. Their terrorist was also openly rude and obstinate while her father was preaching, and he even set up a man to make a choice that would change seven-year-old Rebecca's life forever.

Rebecca forgave the man who changed the course of her life. She forgave the unthinkable not necessarily for the man who eventually sought her forgiveness but for herself. She writes,

> Make no mistake about it. People are observing you and me to see how we, as Christians, deal with the hard knocks of life. When they see that we've been wronged, offended, wounded, ripped off, short-changed, or "done a wrong turn," our response can either attract those who are watching us to the Savior or give them yet another excuse not to follow Him.[1]

At the end of the day, isn't this the best way to show Jesus to the world? A popular writer's adage is "Show, don't tell." This is also the best way to share Jesus with others—show, don't tell.

5. When we forgive, we love our neighbor as ourselves. Yes, it's true forgiveness is more for ourselves than for our offender. Yet we can't discount the benefit to our offender, either. Let's think for just a moment about a time when you have hurt someone you care about. When you heard the words "I forgive you," how did that make you feel? Like a weight had been lifted off of your shoulders? If you haven't yet heard them, how do you think it would make you feel? I don't know about you but it feels good to hear I've been forgiven even after God has released me.

Choosing to forgive is loving our neighbor as ourselves because we have a desire to be forgiven as well. If we want to be forgiven, then we have to forgive. This doesn't mean we need to be best friends with who we are forgiving (we'll talk about this in the next chapter), but it does mean we need to forgive her. The golden rule applies to forgiveness as well!

But what if you haven't heard the words "I forgive you"? You don't need to stand in the chasm of someone else's unforgiveness. Your freedom is not contingent upon how long it takes for someone to forgive you. In fact, when someone you have offended withholds forgiveness, it can some-times be a power struggle or a way to "make you pay" for what you have done. This is incongruent with what we are taught in the Bible, and it's just plain unhealthy. To allow someone with this mind-set to determine your freedom is dangerous business because it gives him or her control rather than God.

I got it all twisted, sister. I allowed my sins, not my Savior, to name my identity; but it's my Savior, not my sins, who says who I am.

6. **We also need to forgive . . . ourselves.** We can't discuss forgiving others without talking about forgiving ourselves as well. I can attest to this one personally, sisters. I've made some choices in my life that weren't great. I've committed offenses that some deem unforgivable. At times, I've hurt those who love me the most. I was one massively imperfect person then and still am now—the difference is I now have Jesus. He lifted me up out of a very dark pit and began the long process of cleaning me up. While I still fall in the mud now and then, I'm able to have much more grace with myself because I know He has it with me.

Yet I also have to forgive myself of those earlier offenses, too. I have to believe I'm a new creation (2 Corinthians 5:17). I must remember that I receive new mercies each day (Lamentations 3:23). I've been washed white as snow (Isaiah 1:18). I am His (Isaiah 43:1). For a while, I walked around with a scarlet letter on my chest. I got it all twisted, sister. I allowed my sins, not my

Savior, to name my identity; but it's my Savior, not my sins, who says who I am.

But then, Jesus came in and set the record straight. He forced me, in a very good way, to root my identity in Him and what He teaches instead of in others and what they thought. My sin no longer defines who I am, and your sin doesn't define who you are. Jesus died for all of it, and when we seek forgiveness from Him with a humble and authentic heart, it's granted.

Here's the other really great thing: we only need to confess and ask forgiveness for a specific offense once. After seeking His forgiveness on multiple occasions for something I had done, it occurred to me that I didn't trust Him to be who He says He is. My own lack of trust was clipping my wings of freedom, and I'm certain God was shaking His head, wondering when the light bulb would illuminate. He doesn't want us to carry around our junk, sisters. One of my favorite verses proves this: "Come to me, all you who are weary and burdened, and I will give you rest. Take my yoke upon you and learn from me, for I am gentle and humble in heart, and you will find rest for your souls. For my yoke is easy and my burden is light" (Matthew 11:28-30).

If you choose to keep carrying your own burdens, just be forewarned: in all likelihood, bitterness, resentment, anger, and a victim mentality will eclipse who you once were. Even worse, it's highly probable those lovely by-products will travel out of your heart and into your words because out of the heart, the mouth speaks. If you want your words to poison, if you desire to give someone else control over your own freedom, and if you want others to start avoiding you, then by all means, refuse to forgive. It will surely accomplish all of these!

All of this talk about forgiveness is great and all, but if you are like I once was, the "how to" part can be a mystery. Sure, you want to forgive. Sure, you don't want to live as a slave to bitterness and resentment, but how do you release the pain you feel when you have been wronged or you've done something to hurt someone else?

1. **Meditate on scriptures about forgiveness.** My favorite verse on forgiveness is Colossians 3:13 (NLT): "Make allowance for each other's faults, and forgive anyone who offends you. Remember, the Lord forgave you, so you must forgive others." Yet another reminder we're called to forgive because we have been forgiven ourselves!

2. **Pray for the one you need to forgive.** Yes, I know this is really, really hard. At first, I had to make myself pray for my enemy, but eventually I realized praying for those who have hurt me actually softened my heart toward them and allowed me to arrive at a state of forgiveness. As mentioned before, sometimes action will precede emotion. "But I tell you, love your enemies and pray for those who persecute you, that you may be children of your Father in heaven" (Matthew 5:44-45).

3. **Mold forgiving children: teach them forgiveness is mandatory in your home.** We will all hurt each other at some point because each of us is disabled by the flesh, but refusing to forgive is denying others of what Jesus so freely gave us. "For if you forgive men when they sin against you, your heavenly Father will also forgive you. But if you do not forgive men their sins, your Father will not forgive your sins" (Matthew 6:14-16).

4. **Imagine your offender as a child.** I know this may seem incredibly weird, but there's something about seeing the sweet, innocent, and pure side of people. They likely played with Barbie

dolls, loved ice cream, and laughed over jokes that didn't make sense. "And he said: 'Truly I tell you, unless you change and become like little children, you will never enter the kingdom of heaven'" (Matthew 18:3).

5. **Ask God to reveal what's at the root of your inability to forgive.** Is it pride? Do you always want to be right? Are you playing a passive-aggressive game that gives you the upper hand as long as you don't forgive? "See, I have refined you, though not as silver; I have tested you in the furnace of affliction. For my own sake, I do this. How can I let myself be defamed? I will not yield my glory to another" (Isaiah 48:10-11).

Forgiveness is a process. Sometimes we will have to choose to forgive for the same offense again. And again. And again. If we were like Jesus, we would forgive just once and move on with our lives. But we're not Jesus—we are disabled by the flesh. That flesh will sometimes allow some of the old feelings of bitterness and resentment to sneak back in and we'll have to make the choice to forgive again. My friend Charlotte was in an abusive marriage a few years ago. She once told me, "Forgiveness is not a one and done thing," and I couldn't agree more! In fact, during my own journey through forgiveness, I have experienced the following stages:

1. **Grief:** Depending on the severity of the offense, we can't be expected to immediately forgive. If you put your foot in your mouth and say something to hurt my feelings, I'll most likely forgive you right then and there. However, God forbid, if a drunk driver were to kill one of my loved ones in an accident, my forgiveness journey might take a bit longer. Yes, it's true Jesus would forgive even that drunk driver right then and there, but remember I'm disabled by the flesh, so I'm likely going to need some time.

Oftentimes, we need a period to grieve the offense committed against us. Though it's true everyone grieves differently, psychologist Elisabeth Kübler-Ross describes five stages of grief in her book titled *On Death and Dying*: denial/isolation, anger, bargaining, depression, and acceptance. These five stages may not be experienced by everyone or in this exact order. Regardless, giving yourself the permission to grieve the loss that results from the offense is part of the forgiveness process.

2. **Make a choice:** You either choose to forgive—or you don't. If you do, you will eventually, if not right away, experience the freedom of forgiveness. It's true there are times when action precedes emotion, so even if you still feel a bit of anger or depression before you forgive, making the choice to forgive will often lead you to the path of complete and authentic forgiveness. If you don't, I can say with complete certainty you will experience the anger, resentment, and bitterness we've been discussing. It's not worth it—God doesn't want you to be held hostage by unforgiveness.

3. **Forgive:** When someone has hurt me, regardless of the magnitude of the offense, I verbally state I have forgiven him or her—even if just in the privacy of my own home. My offender doesn't have to seek my forgiveness because forgiveness is for me.

4. **Experience freedom:** There will be a sense of a weight lifting from your shoulders when you choose to forgive. It's the best part of forgiveness! But . . .

5. **Forgive again:** Depending on the severity of the offense, you might need to choose to forgive again. It's possible you'll need to remind yourself you have already forgiven the offender because forgiveness is a process. Just as God doesn't expect

us to work on every single area of our brokenness at once, He knows there are stages to this forgiveness thing as well. A friend of mine was molested by her father as a child. Through her own forgiveness journey, she forgave her father for violating her. Later, she forgave him of stealing her innocence. Later still, she released herself from any sexual dysfunction that may have resulted from the abuse.

During the forgiveness process, it's possible to vacillate between forgiveness, freedom, and forgiving again. Be patient with yourself as you are walking this path. Remember the best part of following Jesus: grace. Give yourself some of it, too.

An unknown source once stated, "He who forgives, ends a quarrel." Choosing to forgive is seeking peace, and according to the Beatitudes, "blessed are the peacemakers for they will be called children of God" (Matthew 5:9). Seeking peace is not necessarily being meek, quiet, and a mat for all to walk upon. It's not about people-pleasing or being a pushover. Instead, seeking peace means choosing relationship over strife. Sometimes peace-seekers and pursuers of healthy relationships might be considered "pot stirrers" by those who don't understand the freedom of living in peace. People who are still bound in chains will often criticize those who have broken free. As long as you are feeling a nudge from God to speak the truth in love, you are encouraged to pursue peace—which makes you a peacemaker.

And that makes you a child of God. Just in case you were wondering.

DISCUSSION QUESTIONS

1. *Have you ever struggled with forgiveness? Have you experienced bitterness or resentment from a lack of forgiveness?*

2. *Reflect upon Anne Lamott's quote "Not forgiving is like drinking rat poison and waiting for the rat to die." What do you think this means? Have you been waiting for the rat to die after drinking the poison yourself?*

3. *What is your favorite scripture on forgiveness?*

4. *Have you ever prayed for someone who has persecuted you? Describe your experience.*

5. *Have you experienced the freedom that comes from forgiveness? If so, what do you think are the benefits of forgiving?*

CHAPTER SIX

BLURRED LINES
Establishing Holy Boundaries

*Don't let anybody make you do something you do
not want to do. Don't allow someone to utter yes for
you while you're still undecided (say "I'll think about
it"). And do not allow anyone to ever tell you that
"No" is not enough. It is. "No" is a complete sentence. Saying no is a right we all have. Use it.*

Anne Lamott

I once lived a life without boundaries. Need a meal tonight?
Sure, I can pop one right in the oven and have it to you in
an hour. Need someone to watch your kids? Lead the next
Bible study? Chaperone a field trip? Yes, yes, and yes! Count
me in! I just wanted everyone to like me, and I certainly didn't
want to make any waves. If there was a problem, surely Super
Natalie would come to the rescue.

Except Super Natalie began to get tired. She snapped at her
children and was less than kind to her husband. He began to
think of her as a grouch. Her children were confused when they
experienced her impatience yet witnessed a plastered smile on

her face when it was time to serve others. Super Natalie needed boundaries because in the name of ministry, the very people she loved the most were suffering. Not to mention she was stressed-out beyond belief.

Can you identify with my alter ego? Thankfully, Super Natalie is a me from the past, although now and then she tries to make an appearance again. What Super Natalie failed to realize is (1) no matter how hard she worked, not everyone was going to like her; (2) serving to the point of exhaustion is not serving in the way in which she was called to serve; and (3) living without boundaries was a poor example for her children and communicated to her husband that he was the last priority on the list. Something had to change.

Boundary is not a dirty word, though there are some who would like you to believe it is (more about that later). In fact, establishing relational boundaries is one of the most loving things you can do for your family and yourself. You cannot control how others will behave, but you can control how you react. Boundaries make this a reality and allow you to handle sticky situations with a grace that would make Mother Teresa proud.

Boundaries come in especially handy when you've had an unresolved conflict with a friend or a family member whom you will need to see on occasion. Hopefully you have forgiven, but just because you have forgiven doesn't mean you feel emotionally safe with the person who hurt you. Boundaries allow you to remain in relationship to a certain extent *and* guard your heart at the same time.

But what exactly are boundaries and how do we establish them? No doubt it takes practice. Like anything else, the more

Have you ever heard of the acronym B.U.S.Y.? Being Under Satan's Yoke. It's true, isn't it? When we are busy we don't have time to focus on what really matters.

we establish relational boundaries, the easier it becomes to hold them in place. Boundaries allow us to:

1. **Define the line so we know when it's been crossed.** It's been said our own personal boundaries are like a fence around our yard. You wouldn't expect someone to walk through your fence uninvited, would you? Boundaries are an unspoken (or sometimes spoken!) line of conduct most people with healthy social understanding will follow.

2. **Maintain our roots in Him.** When we are rooted in God and commit to following Jesus, we no longer allow the world to identify who we are. Instead, we are identified by who Jesus says we are, and because of our love for the Lord, we desire to live how He wants us to live. Anything that is outside the parameters of how God wants us to live can jeopardize our relationship with Him.

3. **Communicate healthy expectations in relationships.** Sometimes our boundaries *do* need to be communicated to others. If personal boundaries are repeatedly crossed, we probably need to talk to who is doing the crossing. Lovingly telling people what to expect leads to a relationship built on respect. The mystery of expectation is removed and no one needs to cry "Awkward!"

4. **Choose not to be overscheduled.** Have you ever heard of the acronym B.U.S.Y.? Being Under Satan's Yoke. It's true, isn't it? When we are busy we don't have time to focus on what

really matters. As was the case with Super Natalie, we can forget our family is our first ministry. When we allow our identity to come from the approval of others, we miss out on living with the joyous approval from God. We believe the lie that our performance will earn our salvation, a higher social standing, or qualify us as Christian of the Year. When we equate a busy schedule with success, we often don't understand why we're more stressed. I've learned this one the hard way, sisters: you will eventually suffer from burnout. When we burn out, we need to prioritize self-care because if we don't, we can't care for anyone else.

When we place boundaries around our schedule, we allow for self-care, and self-care is critical if we are going to do anything God has called us to do. We are indeed God's handiwork, and He's created good works for us to do in advance; however, He didn't create us to do *all* of the good works (Ephesians 2:10). In addition, He wants us to be cheerful givers (2 Corinthians 9:7), but we can't be too cheerful when we are exhausted and suffering from burnout! Rest is critical if we are to thrive, but it won't happen unless we establish boundaries around our schedule and learn to say one very short word: no.

5. Take care of ourselves. Rest is crucial, and this doesn't mean just getting enough sleep. This also means not overcommitting and running from point A to point B like a chicken without a head! Self-care also means eating the right foods, exercising, and spending time with those who encourage you and love you for who you are. During His time on earth, Jesus understood this need. He knew He would need to pull away from the crowds even when there was still work to be done so He could rest. He knew He would need to slow down long enough to eat a good meal, and He knew when He felt like He needed time with His Father. When we don't take care of our own physical and emotional needs, we can't give from our overflow because there simply isn't any overflow to give.

6. **Discern appropriate behavior.** When we are rooted in Him and understand His boundaries for us, we have a keener gauge of what is appropriate and what is not. For example, at our house we have a boundary around the television shows our children watch. My three children have learned what constitutes appropriate and inappropriate television, so it's become easy for them to discern when a show is fine to watch and when it's not. This is important to us as a family because we want our children to make the decision to watch shows that guard their hearts even when we as parents are not present. Without this boundary, they leave their hearts exposed to material they may not yet be emotionally ready to see.

7. **Speak the truth in love.** When we are rooted in Him and we understand the source of our worth, speaking the truth in love becomes a little easier. Earlier, we discussed the story told in Matthew 19 about the rich, young man seeking knowledge of how to gain eternal life. Due to Jesus' boundaries of following instruction from His heavenly Father, He was able to tell the young man the truth: if he wanted to gain entry into heaven, he had to sell his possessions and give to the poor. Though it was difficult for this young man to hear, Jesus was able to speak the truth in love because of His own knowledge of what is acceptable to God. At the same time, I know there have been moments in my life when I didn't know what I didn't know. I have felt certain I had done nothing wrong in a given situation only to find, even years later, I actually had been wrong. Luckily, there's grace for

being human. We will make mistakes. The seeds of our mistake eventually bloom into the fruit of wisdom!

As with humility and grace, boundaries are also essential to healthy relationships as well. You simply cannot be expected to fulfill all of the needs the world suggests you should fulfill because the truth is, it's not humanly possible. Boundaries are the antidote to a life that is harried, overscheduled, and stressful. At the same time, there is a dangerous misconception about boundaries, especially within the Christian community. After all, aren't we supposed to love all? Accept all? Forgive repeatedly? Yes, yes, and yes. Sometimes the most loving thing we can do is to place boundaries around a relationship. In addition, it's entirely possible to integrate a boundary and forgive at the same time. Remember: forgiveness is for you—not necessarily for your offender. Since we've already discussed what boundaries *are*, let's take a look at what they *are not* by examining the four "uns":

1. Boundaries are not unkind. Boundaries are not only healthy, they're holy. As we discussed earlier, Jesus understood His own human limitations. He retreated often to rest and pray. He understood when He needed to eat. He spent time in silence when He needed to grieve or just be still. Jesus chose to live inside out—He ministered to His soul *inside* so what poured *outside* was good. In the past, I have lived outside in, which is, of course, completely the opposite. I prioritized others over the needs of my family and myself, and I gave the outside world permission to identify who I am. Lack of boundaries can make you forget who you are and whose you are.

When someone is prioritizing her well-being, do you think she's being unkind? It sounds funny to say it this way, doesn't it? Of course she isn't being unkind—she's being wise! When we say yes to something, we're saying no to something else. Are we repeatedly saying no to our families? Is this unkind? Yes! However, in the same vein, is it unkind to say no to something because it wouldn't be best for our families? Absolutely not! You have established a holy boundary because God has entrusted you to care for your family and He expects you to prioritize their needs most of the time. Now and then, there might be opportunities to help and serve others, unusual occasions that interfere with family life, but this isn't what I'm talking about. I'm talking about the repeated choosing to help others in the name of ministry at the expense of your own family.

In addition, when we say no to accepting something we've been asked to do, we give someone else who genuinely might be interested in the task at hand a chance to rise up and do it. So often, my own pride made me feel as though I had to say yes to everything I was asked to do because I was the only one who could do it right. I was once asked to mentor a young woman in our community, and without spending much time in prayer, I accepted the opportunity because I was flattered to have been asked. In the end, I was too overscheduled to com-mit to meeting with her on a regular basis. If I had examined my commitments more accurately, she could have moved on her merry way and found someone who would have been able to spend more time with her. I needed to *get out* of the way of myself so others could *get in* to serve. Who knows? Maybe the opportunity to help would have been drudgery for you but com-plete joy for the person who was meant to do it. When this hap-pens, the kingdom will benefit because we were wise enough to place a boundary and get out of the way—of ourselves.

2. Boundaries are not un-Christian. Having held leadership positions within the church, I've had many expectations placed upon my shoulders. Admittedly, I put some of those expectations there myself; however, that was not always the case. Regardless, it was expected I would always be Super Natalie because I was a Christian—and a Christian in leadership at that. Nice girls in leadership don't say no. Even when I stepped down from leadership positions within the church, I still experienced these expectations due to the public nature of my blog. When I didn't pursue a relationship to the extent the person wanted to be pursued, I became a phony. When I made a mistake, there seemed to be much less grace and I was accused of being unbiblical. When I said no to anything good, it was a rare occasion when someone said, "Good for you for looking out for yourself!" Instead, I was often met with criticism and that criticism usually suggested my boundaries were un-Christian.

Again, boundaries are not only healthy—they're holy. During a particularly difficult time, I was directed to one of my favorite chapters of the Bible: Psalm 62:7 says, "My salvation and my honor depend on God; he is my mighty rock, my refuge." Your honor comes from the Lord and not your critics. When you are keeping your eyes on the cross and know you are undoubtedly hearing His direction, then you're being obedient to Him if you feel a nudge to put boundaries in place. There's nothing un-Christian about that, sisters. Far from it.

Yet it's true we all need to check our hearts when we use the term *boundary* in our friendships. My friend Mandy recently confided in me that she has another friend who used the term *boundary* for her own advantage. In a nutshell, Mandy felt this term was used to keep everything on her friend's terms with complete disregard for her own feelings. Boundaries are a tool for our protection, but they are not to be used as an excuse to make the friendship all about ourselves and always get our own way. Nor are they an excuse to refuse forgiveness or reconciliation. That's giving pride the upper hand, and pride will take you down a long, lonely road. In the end, we need to check our own hearts and be sure our motives for establishing boundaries are pure.

3. **Boundaries are not ungrateful.** When we place boundaries in a relationship, we aren't suggesting we are not grateful for what the other person has done or is doing. We are prioritizing the protection of our hearts. The healthy guarding of our hearts shields us from continuous hurts.

Sometimes, those who have hurt us will continue to try to hurt us by covert aggressive criticism or disrespect. I have a friend whose ex-husband repeatedly puts her down to their children. While my friend is grateful for her ex-husband's role in her children's lives, she also speaks the truth to them when she is asked about the lies they are told. She has decided instead to forgive him (even when it's hard), pray he will stop putting her down, and lovingly speak truth to her children in the meantime. She has established holy boundaries to protect the truth.

On the flip side, it's also important we're supporting others' boundaries as well. When someone says she can't do something you want her to do, the best response is "I'm sorry you can't _____, but good for you for honoring your boundaries!" Guilt trips can make those who have chosen holy boundaries feel as though they're doing wrong instead of mirroring Jesus by understanding their own limitations. I've experienced this firsthand and I'm guessing you have as well. Be forewarned: there are steamrollers out there that just want to get their own way. They might try to run you over, but the more practice you have with setting boundaries, the less likely they are to flatten you.

Don't be shocked if not everyone reacts to your newfound freedom obtained through forgiveness and boundaries with the same excitement as you. You know the saying "Misery loves company" don't you? There's a bit of truth to it. When your light starts to shine brighter, it can illuminate the darkness in the souls of others. Not everyone wants to see their own darkness because facing the deep and ugly trenches of our own hearts can be terrifying. There are many who live with this darkness be-cause (1) they don't know any other way of living; (2) they don't realize they are being held captive by their own darkness; and (3) it's easier than confronting what placed the darkness there in the first place.

People might be jealous of you because they want what you've got and don't realize they can have it as well. It's also possible they don't want you to start living better because it means they might be encouraged to do so as well—and some people are just fine being miserable. When someone else's sin becomes our own through transference from one person to another, I call it "contagious sin." A few years ago, I was friends with a woman who needed to control every situation. She needed to dictate when we would get together, what we would do, and who would be involved. She pretty much needed to be in charge of all details, and if anyone else dared to take over, watch out. In complete rebellion, I soon found myself wanting to not go along with her plan. Her control was rooted in fear, and I allowed her sin to become my sin. It was contagious sin. It was still my choice to act the way I did; we can't blame anyone else for our choices but ourselves. In the end, it's true we are all broken and we need to have compassion with others who are broken; however, this doesn't mean we should compromise our own health just so someone else can feel OK about herself.

In fact, author Marianne Williamson illustrates this concept beautifully by stating,

> Our deepest fear is not that we are inadequate. Our deepest fear is that we are powerful beyond measure. It is our light, not our darkness that most frightens us. We ask ourselves, "Who am I to be brilliant, gorgeous, talented, fabulous?" Actually, who are you not to be? You are a child of God. Your playing small does not serve the world. There is nothing enlightened about shrinking so that other people won't feel insecure around you. We are all meant to shine, as children do. We were born to make manifest the glory of God that is within us. It's not just in some of us; it's in everyone. And as we let our own light shine, we unconsciously give other people permission to do the same. As we are liberated from our own fear, our presence automatically liberates others.[1]

Don't dim your light, sisters. Shine it brightly—it was purchased at a very high price. Pray for the person who is threatened by your growth and erect a boundary to stop the contagious sin.

4. Boundaries are not unhealthy. Proverbs 4:23 tells us to guard our hearts "above all else . . . for it is the wellspring of life." When we place boundaries around unhealthy relationships, we're guarding our hearts. If we are to love God with all of our heart and soul and also love our neighbor as ourselves, then we better take good care of our own hearts so we can! Hence why it is stated "above all else" in the Bible because God knew the heart would need to be cared for first and foremost.

Out of the heart, the mouth speaks (Luke 6:45). Our words have the power to murder or minister. A hurting heart uses words to murder by putting you down, making you feel unworthy, and being covertly aggressive. Sometimes, that person is just jealous of you or threatened by your newfound freedom and wish you would just dim your light already. If this is the case with any of your relationships, you can still be loving and kind but you don't have to continue to expose your own heart to negativity.

While we're on this subject of unhealthy relationships, allow me to share some of the wisdom I've obtained while getting my PhD in people-pleasing. As a recovered people pleaser, I know all too well about the pitfalls of allowing others to identify my self-worth. As my beloved eighty-nine-year-old Meemo says, "Not everyone is going to like you." Meemo's right—there are people out there who won't like you simply because of the way you look. They might smack an unfounded and unfair label on you. You might sometimes be judged incorrectly. Some struggle with giving grace, and a small mistake will be held over your head. It's possible you might be the object of someone's own jealousy and insecurity, and that person is just waiting to find something to attack. I know this might sound harsh, but I've experienced each of these instances, and I'm guessing you may have had some experience with a few of these yourself. Don't waste your precious energy trying to win over someone who is committed to misunderstanding you. Being the lover of quotes that I am, one of my favorites on this topic was spoken by Theodore Roosevelt in his speech "Citizens in a Republic." President Roosevelt stated,

It is not the critic who counts; not the man who points out how the strong man stumbles, or where the doer of deeds could have done them better. The credit belongs to the man who is actually in the arena, whose face is marred by dust and sweat and blood; who strives valiantly; who errs, who comes short again and again, because there is no effort without error and shortcoming; but who does actually strive to do the deeds; who knows great enthusiasms, the great devotions; who spends himself in a worthy cause; who at the best knows in the end the triumph of high achievement, and who at the worst, if he fails, at least fails while daring greatly, so that his place shall never be with those cold and timid souls who neither know victory nor defeat.[2]

I don't know about you, but even when it gets tough and I feel like I'm continually being persecuted, I would still rather be in the arena with a face covered in dust, sweat, and blood regardless of what anyone else might say.

WHEN AND HOW: ESTABLISHING BOUNDARIES IN UNHEALTHY RELATIONSHIPS

While you may want to react to those who attack you from your own flesh, I would suggest you dig in deep for a dose of self-control and handle their hurt with grace. Yet another lesson I've learned the hard way, sisters. When we get defensive, we give the offender exactly what he or she is seeking: (1) proof that you aren't who you say you are, (2) proof that he or she has the power to get under your skin, and (3) proof you can be relied upon to be a source of drama. There's no denying the fact there are people out there who prefer drama over peace. Graham Cooke calls these people "grace growers" because that's exactly what they do for us: they give us opportunities to grow more grace with others.[3] But if our grace growers don't get what they want, they'll eventually get bored and look for another victim who's a little more fun and willing to play their game.

Yet when this messy stuff happens, it's important to examine our own hearts as well. Psalm 139 says, "Search me, O God, and know my heart; test me and know my anxious thoughts. Point out anything in me that offends you, and lead me along the path of everlasting life" (vv. 23-24 NLT). If we are reacting to the naysayers in our lives with bitterness and anger, then we need to reassess where we are in the forgiveness process and consider releasing them. While my words regarding those who may be against you might sound a bit harsh, I'm not suggesting you treat those who persecute you with anything less than grace—even when it's hard. Flinging back will ignite the flame, but grace is a mighty extinguisher.

Since knowing when to establish boundaries can be tricky, we can sometimes be at a loss for what to do in a challenging relationship. A relationship might be crying out for boundaries if:

1. The offender repeatedly mistreats you and makes indirect, biting remarks so they don't seem so bad, but their intent is to take you down a bit. (Covert Aggression)
2. There is an obvious lack of humility when you attempt to talk about your own hurt with her.
3. She repeatedly spins the issue so you leave the conversation feeling that it's you in the wrong and never her.

A life without bound-aries is a life with chaos, confusion, and craziness.

4. You notice you're consistently feeling beaten down rather than built up when you leave her company.

5. She doesn't have your best inter-est at heart—just her own. She has an "all about me" mind-set.

As we begin to stick our toes in the waters of establishing boundaries, it's normal to experience a few challenges. As is the case with anything we are trying to do to improve our lives, we need to have grace with ourselves during this journey. In fact, we usually identify the need for change when we assess what isn't working so well. Common boundary mistakes include:

1. **No boundaries at all:** Life is in a constant state of chaos when no boundaries exist. Children go to bed when they want. Dinner is eaten whenever everyone is hungry, and then it's everyone fending for himself or herself. Calls are taken during family time, and people stop over unannounced. Friends and family dump their problems off at all hours of the day and expect you to be there. Not having boundaries leads to chaos, confusion, and most of all, exhaustion. A life without boundaries is a life with chaos, confusion, and craziness.

2. **Not communicating boundaries:** I once found myself in a tough situation with a friend, and it became obvious I would need to put some boundaries in place within our relationship. I felt I needed to retreat a bit so I could re-center and hear from God about this particular friendship. The problem was that I didn't communicate this to my friend. She felt abandoned and

hurt that I had pulled away so abruptly and, in retrospect, I completely understand why. I should have communicated to her that I needed some space to sort through a few issues. Instead, I took the coward's way out and didn't address it at all because I knew it would be a tough conversation. When others know where our boundaries lie, then they can more easily respect them. However, if we play a guessing game with them, then it becomes just that—a game. Emotional games are not only unhealthy—they're unkind.

3. **Inconsistent Boundaries:** Here today, gone tomorrow. This is a field of boundary land mines! When we integrate a boundary one day but don't follow it the next, we leave everyone, including ourselves, scratching their heads and wondering how to proceed. If we engage in gossip one day but refuse to do so the next, it's unclear where we stand with this. Not to mention that eventually, resentment builds against the one establishing the inconsistent boundaries because no one ever knows their expectations.

4. **Inflexible boundaries:** I don't believe life is always black and white. It's true there are times when relational boundaries should be lifted for the sake of common courtesy. Several years ago, a person who had repeatedly wronged a friend of mine said hello to her at a public venue. My friend returned his greeting. It was a beautiful example of behavior-grace. "I can't compromise courtesy and make the conflict worse by lack of maturity. While I'm not going to engage him in conversation, I can respond when he's spoken to me because I'm not going to repay evil with evil," my friend said later when I was applauding how she handled the situation. Amazing grace, indeed. She refused to allow the sin to be contagious.

5. Inappropriate boundaries: Please allow me to be bold and state something that isn't always so popular to proclaim: I don't believe married men and women can be intimate friends with anyone of the opposite gender. In fact, I personally believe it's nowhere near appropriate to open our hearts to a person of the opposite gender other than our spouses. Allow me to explain.

My friend Susan described her relationship with a male colleague as a "very close friend." She went to him for advice, sought him for fun, and depended on him to cheer her when she was having a rough day. Susan eventually became emotionally dependent upon her male colleague—but she was married to someone else. She consistently sought from another man what only her husband should have given her, and they became emotionally connected. When Susan's colleague retreated from their friendship, she was shattered.

The more I talked with my friend about this relationship, the clearer it became: she had an ungodly soul tie with her colleague, and it wasn't healthy. Soul ties are defined as any emotional connection your own soul has with another person's soul. These are usually the first people we seek when something goes awry in our own lives. They have the power to stir up both intensely positive emotions as well as downright negative emotions within us. In addition, they have a tremendous amount of influence over us. As is so often the case with soul ties, someone is looking for the other person to fulfill what only God or a spouse is meant to fulfill.

Marriages can experience valleys that leave both spouses feeling confused, hurt, and hopeless. My husband and I have been there and we know we will be again—it's simply the nature of marriage. However, if we ever choose to develop a friendship with a member of the opposite gender, we make it that much easier to muddy the waters and cross the line from platonic relationship to romantic relationship. I know not everyone agrees with me on this, but we live in an age where extramarital affairs are not all that unusual. I'm not suggesting we can't talk to anyone of the opposite gender because that's not realistic. Platonic *relationships* with the opposite gender are different from a platonic *friendship*. For example, it's normal for men and women to interact in the workplace; however, you will likely have a different boundary with your male colleagues than you would your female colleagues. If you work closely with a man on the job, it's a good idea to not rely on him to fulfill any of your emotional needs and to get to know or at least be acquainted with his spouse (if he has one).

Most affairs occur because two people have not maintained appropriate boundaries between one another. In these conditions, it's far easier to stray when their marriage walks through the inevitable valley. I do have platonic relationships; however, they're the spouses of my Heart Sisters, and I would never seek them out to meet me for dinner or join me at the mall. I spend time with them only when their wives are present. Living above reproach will protect our emotional connections with our own spouses and show other women you are trustworthy.

Establishing boundaries can be like training for a marathon. The training period can be difficult. You'll have bad runs and good runs. You'll be tired at times, and you might be inconsistent now and then. Luckily, there is grace. I think most marathoners will tell you that the training can be grueling yet there's not a better feeling than crossing the finish line. The same is true once you get the hang of setting boundaries: you won't believe the freedom you'll feel!

DISCUSSION QUESTIONS

1. What do you first think of when you hear the word boundaries?

2. What is your biggest challenge with establishing boundaries?

3. Are there any areas of your life that need boundaries? How can you establish them?

4. How do you think boundaries can decrease stress?

5. What are your thoughts about soul ties?

CHAPTER SEVEN

TEXTING, TWITTER, AND TUMBLR

Friendship Etiquette in a Digital World

> *In my opinion, all previous advances in the various lines of invention will appear totally insignificant when compared with those which the present century will witness. I almost wish that I might live my life over again to see the wonders which are at the threshold.*
> Charles Holland Duell, Commissioner of the United States Patent and Trademark Office, 1898–1901

The wonders Charles Duell spoke of likely far exceed his wildest dreams! Honestly, so many developments in technology exceed my own wildest dreams, and I've been alive to watch most of them come into fruition. Allow me to have my own I-walked-a-mile-to-school-every-day-in-three-feet-of-snow moment: there was no Internet when I was in college.

Currently living in a college town, we are blessed to have many options of babysitters for our children. Recently, I shared this tidbit of trivia with one of them, and you would have thought I said we traveled to class in a horse and buggy. It was unfathomable to her. "How did you write papers?" she asked. The story took on a whole new level of hilarity when I told her about walking across campus to the library and paying ten cents to print off articles from microfilm. Explaining microfilm was even funnier. According to the Beloit College Mindset List, a list of characteristics of incoming college freshmen as a generational comparison, our current college freshmen have never known a suitcase not to have wheels. GM means food that is genetically modified. The have known only two presidents. They have never attended a concert in a smoke-filled arena. The biblical sources of terms such as "forbidden fruit," "the writing on the wall," "good Samaritan," and "the Promised Land" are unknown to most of them.

Technology has changed the tone of our culture—for better or worse, like it or not. While it's true certain technologies allow us to gain access to material that can lead to sin more readily and easily than if it didn't exist (think pornography), I believe it's neutral in terms of its good and evil. Technology is a tool in which this good and evil is dependent upon the one holding the controls—the user. When we choose to use technology, be it e-mail, Facebook, or texting, we have a responsibility to use this tool wisely. A hammer was intended to be used to pound in nails. However, it can also be used to hit someone over the head, too. How we use the tool determines its goodness or evil.

Social media and other avenues of technology, like e-mail and texting, are popular because of the way God has wired (pardon the pun) each of us: to connect and communicate with others. We can't interact with each other if we don't communicate, right? Back when I was a child, if you wanted to connect with someone, you did so through a snail mail letter, telephone call (using a telephone with a cord, mind you), or in person. Today, I can connect with thousands of people by simply hitting a button. We live in an age where communication can occur immediately. While in some instances this is a very helpful fact of life, in other cases, it's the bullet that shoots right through the foot. Social media requires social graces.

Let's first look at the drawbacks of using technology. When we don't place boundaries around our personal technology usage, the tool can be used negatively instead of positively. If not monitored, technology can:

1. Reduce the amount of time we spend interacting with those around us. It used to be if I were waiting in a line, someone would strike up a conversation. I enjoy talking with strangers because I've actually met a few in-real-life friends this way! While I realize not everyone shares the same sentiment, there's something to be said for the dying art of a spoken conversation. We learn to take turns. We learn to inquire about the other person. We hear other perspectives. Now, if I'm waiting in a line, most faces are turned toward their smartphones, interacting with the digital world rather than the real world around them.

Hear me on this, too: there is no condemnation if you are identifying yourself here. I'm usually one of the people with my head down using my smartphone, too. But I have to wonder if this lack of interacting with the people around us is contributing to an increase in the feeling of disconnect in our relationships. I've seen what can be accomplished through the simple act of healthy conversation—it's the only way we will ever be able to disagree with one another respectfully and hear the other side.

2. Spread lies more efficiently. Mark Twain is reported to have said, "A lie can travel halfway around the world while the truth is putting on its shoes." Let's face it: lies are often a bit juicier than the actual truth, right? Juiciness leads to gossip, and gossip can spread like wildfire. On the other hand, the truth is often not as exciting as the spiced-up version. Exaggeration is the same as a lie—when we exaggerate, we're embellishing. We are dressing up our lives to sound more exciting, often because we think we'll be valued more if we have a pretty front porch. Social media can lead us to exaggerate, embellish, and expand the truth.

Scandal sells, and the media embellishes most of these scandals to increase the sales of newspapers and magazines. My daughter's teacher found something on Pinterest and posted it in her classroom. I "think" it is helpful for us all: Before you speak, T.H.I.N.K! Is it True? Is it Helpful? Is it Inspiring? Is it Necessary? Is it Kind? These same criteria should be met when posting to social media.

3. Be addictive. We are faced with an issue that didn't concern us last decade: constant accessibility. While smartphones have their advantages, it's true they have added a new level of stress and many of us aren't even aware they're the culprit. When we all carried around traditional cell phones (or dumbphones, as I've heard they are called now), we couldn't check our e-mail. We could simply make and receive calls and, now and then, send a text message, but it often took too long so we seldom did.

Yet now, it's possible for someone to reach me at all times— with the exception of when I am asleep during the night. In fact, I've noticed a shift in our own expectations as a culture. Before smartphones, it wasn't a big deal to respond to an e-mail after two or even three days. However, now it seems if I wait a few days before responding, I'm met with "Didn't you get my e-mail?" Of course, I have gotten their message, but I also have a finite amount of time to work with, and that's true of us all. I don't prioritize technology unless it's an absolute emergency, and this can sometimes offend people because our culture now expects an immediate response.

Author Edward Hallowell says, "The great thing about modern life is you can do so much and the curse of modern life is you can do so much."[1] It used to be we checked our e-mail once a day, and now it's common for people to check their in-boxes up to thirty times an hour. Yes. Thirty times an hour. "There's something very irresistible about an unopened message," Hallowell says. "You do get a dopamine squirt from accessing your messages. The mail used to come once a day. Now it comes every second."[2] The invention of smartphones has given more people more job flexibility, but if boundaries aren't in place, a good thing can quickly become bad.

Like Pavlov's dogs, many of us have been trained to run to our phones when we hear the double buzz of an incoming text or the ding of a new, unread message. In full disclosure, I admit that my own technology usage has interfered with my family time and has taken away attention that should have been focused on what matters to me the most: God, my husband, and my children. When we are constantly connected without any boundaries, our brains get addicted to the visual output and we begin to panic when it's gone.

Two years ago, I was blessed to go to Ghana with my friends Dana and Rachel. If you want to go through a quick rehabilitation

When we close the door on distractions for a period of time, we open the door to hearing from God.

of technology, go to Africa! The cost to use our smartphones was so great it was better to not use them during the ten days we were in Ghana. The first two days were very strange—what was going on? Did someone need me? Did someone want to contact me? What's happening in the world? What if something happens to my family? It was then I realized the truth behind our greatest need as humans: to feel wanted and needed. This desire can be addictive when it's channeled toward something other than God. We soon begin to place our identity in the amount of e-mails and texts we receive instead of seeking our value in Him.

Something magical began to happen after those first two days in Ghana. I looked around to see natives who were filled with joy beyond imagination—and by our standards, they had nothing. A group of boys playing soccer with a balloon were spilling contagious laughter into the streets. I sat down and had real conversations. I listened to the hearts of others instead of hearing bits and pieces around my distractions. I watched children having a ball playing hopscotch with just a rock and the course drawn in the dirt with their fingers.

While these experiences weren't what I would consider to be the best part of unplugging, they're a close second. The best part of limiting my accessibility was I found myself talking to God more often. And get this—I was getting much better at hearing Him. If we're constantly plugged in, it becomes harder to unplug. It's the whole rest-to-serve-others-best concept. So often, the "other" you are serving first is yourself. When we close the door on distractions for a period of time, we open the door to hearing from God. What's the point if we are living our lives without listening to Him? If we rely on technology to feel wanted and needed, we need to go back to God and be treated.

How can we wean ourselves off our technology addiction? By remembering to live in the P.R.E.S.E.N.T.:

1. Prioritize: What is important to you? Do you need to check your messages during your child's school play, or can it wait for an hour? Are family dinners or time spent with friends important? What are your rules concerning technology during mealtimes?

2. Rest: While it's true our bodies need an average of eight hours of sleep each night to rejuvenate and refresh our energy and foster new cell growth, our brains also need periods of rest throughout the day. Perhaps this is the reason why Europeans often close their businesses during the afternoon hours so they can refresh, clear their minds, and serve their customers more effectively.

3. Ease in: Don't try to go cold turkey on this, friends! Just because you are trying to switch the way you use technology from that of a lifeline to a tool doesn't mean you have to stop all usage. However, if technology has become an idol (anything you place above God), then you might consider this until you feel as if you are again right with God. Most of all, have grace with yourself. If you mess up and check your e-mail thirty times in an hour, there's a new hour coming.

4. Set boundaries: This is critical, sisters. Put your phone away when you are spending time with someone you love. When you choose to text and talk on the phone while you are with another person, it can be hurtful to him or her because that person has prioritized time to be with you. Designate specific times to check your e-mail. Refuse to allow technology to distract you from in-real-life relationships. See technology for the tool it is rather than the lifeline it's become. And turn your phone off during the night so you can rest more effectively.

5. Explain: If you find others chiding you about your limitations on technology, you might need to explain why you have chosen to place boundaries around your time. Whereas I don't believe we have to explain our choices to others outside of our immediate family, I do believe that others are more apt to respect your boundaries if they are aware of why you have put them in place, especially if you are fully present when you are with them.

6. Never make others feel guilty: If someone hasn't returned your e-mail, there's a way to ask her if she received it that won't put her on the offensive. It's all about tone on this one, friends. "Did you get my message?" can sound either inquiring or accusing depending on how you choose to say it. Also, give grace with reply time—life happens. Who knows what kind of week the person you've contacted has had? If she is prioritizing God and her family first, she's walking within His boundaries for her. That's obedience, and we need to applaud that rather than add another layer of guilt.

7. Type away! If you have taken all of the above precautions, you should be ready to use technology as a tool and not a lifeline. However, if you ever find yourself struggling with it again, you can begin the P.R.E.S.E.N.T. process over from the start.

While technology can certainly be a bad thing, let's not discount the fact that as with any tool, it can also be used for good. The tool's demeanor is dependent upon the user—we are those users. Technology's advantages include:

1. It enables us to share our faith with more people. Technology often gives us a platform to share our beliefs. We can post Facebook status updates to encourage others. We can check in with people via Twitter. We can start a blog and share our faith. Technology enlarges our territory to speak the truth in love, but we must be aware of our own words even if our hearts are pure. We'll discuss etiquette of this in the next section.

2. It's quicker and more efficient. It's true if we want to make plans to meet friends at a restaurant for a much-needed girls' night out, technology makes this far easier to plan than having to coordinate everyone's schedules via telephone. In fact, as we'll discuss in the next section, technology is used at its best to make plans and communicate trivial details.

3. It has given us more flexibility and efficiency within our jobs. Technology has allowed working from home to be an option for many who are now able to have a better quality of life and use their time more effectively. This being said, if firm boundaries aren't in place, it's easy to allow technology to seep into our family life and muddy the waters of work time and family time. Again, technology is a tool, and it's up to us to determine how we use it.

So how should we use technology in a way that honors and glorifies God and encourages others? Remember, "What you say flows from what is in your heart" (Luke 6:45 NLT). Your heart can be represented by what you write as well. If we are to use technology responsibly, we will need to be cognizant of what we decide to publish. Besides our words, there are decisions we will have to make, such as when to unfriend someone or how to respond to a biting e-mail message. Read on, technology warrior.

I have made my own fair share of errors while navigating the world of technology. I'm pretty sure we all have at least one horror story! In fact, I remember a time early on when e-mail was relatively new and I spoke not so nicely about a man I had previously dated. You guessed it—the message was sent to him along with my two other friends. Not one of my prouder moments, for sure.

We all make mistakes, and there is forgiveness-grace; however, we need to strive to handle e-mails, text messages, Facebook, and blogs with behavior-grace. Sounding off and being quick to anger will detract others and put your credibility in danger. This not only hurts you but the kingdom of God as well. Because while your heart may be pure and have good intentions, your method of communicating truth might not be peppered with enough love. The balance of grace and truth is a fine, but very necessary, line to straddle. So let's discuss some of the more common technologies and the etiquette for each, shall we?

1. E-mail: E-mail is great for communicating plans and messages without emotion. Deciding on where and when to meet for dinner is within the scope of responsible e-mail usage as well as other trivial bits of information, like what chapters we are reading for book club. However, e-mail is not the place to share your deepest, darkest concerns with another person. It's tempting to do this since choosing to communicate via e-mail subtracts the face-to-face contact with the person you are confronting from the equation. But, in the end, we show a higher regard for the recipient of our concerns if we speak to her in person.

Using e-mail to confront potentially emotional conversations is dangerous because (1) the listener can't read your body language or your tone of voice; (2) your words can be forwarded on to others in a quick, emotional response from your recipient; and (3) intentions can be misconstrued since the person sending the message is not present to answer questions.

But what if *you* are the one receiving a zinger of a message? First, resist the urge to share it with others. I know you might want to glean other perspectives and seek wise counsel, but take a deep breath and wait. Second, here's another lesson I've learned from the school of hard knocks: don't respond right away. Follow the P.E.G. System we discussed in chapter 4: pray, examine, and go. However, if you decide you must go and delve deeper into the issue, I would caution you in doing so by e-mail. If you do, make it a short and simple response such as, "Thank you for sharing your hurt with me. I would like to talk with you about this further, but I want to talk in person. When could we meet?" Or, just pick up the telephone.

Speaking of wise counsel, we are told in James 1:5 if we lack wisdom, we just need to ask God to give it to us and He will. However, sometimes He imparts this wisdom through others. Similarly, Proverbs 12:15 says, "The way of fools seems right to them, but the wise listen to advice." I have been a fool and done what seems right only to find I probably should have sought the counsel of wise friends. However, notice what kind of friends we should seek. Wise friends. We must be extremely cautious in who we choose to seek for wise counsel because when we choose to follow Jesus, we begin to live by a different set of standards. When we seek a nonbeliever for wise counsel, we may not receive biblically based wisdom. I'm not suggesting those who don't believe can't dispense good advice, but I am saying they may not always give advice that would be in alignment with God's plan.

2. Facebook: I love Facebook. I have reconnected with so many people from my past, and it's widened the scope of those with whom I interact regularly. This being said, I've noticed it can also be another avenue in which we can be hurt if it's not used respectfully. Just the other day, my daughter was sharing a story with me about a young girl who continuously threatens to revoke her friendship if my daughter doesn't do what she wants her to do. In a nutshell, this young woman is trying to manipulate Sarah in the hope of being able to run the show. If Sarah doesn't play by her rules, then this little girl won't be her friend.

Lo and behold, there came a day when Sarah didn't want to play what her friend was playing. For two days, her friend didn't speak to her—she stood by her threat of no longer being my daughter's friend. Sarah tried to speak to her about this, but her friend refused. After my mama-bear self settled down, I was able to have some really great discussions with Sarah about establishing boundaries within friendships and the qualities good friends possess. However, she was hurt. She felt as if she had been punished for simply not wanting to do what someone else wanted her to do. She had been unfriended in real life and with little explanation.

I have heard countless stories about a friend getting angry at another friend and one of them unfriends the other on Facebook. Unfriending is akin to saying "I'm cutting you out of my life" and so often, it's making a statement to the source of her anger. It's the big girl's way of threatening someone to revoke her friendship if she doesn't go along with her rules. There are indeed moments when unfriending someone is a good choice in regard to guarding and protecting your heart. Yet I've also experienced the rash decision of being unfriended, and it's especially hurtful when it's from someone you thought was a good friend but would rather flee the scene than talk it through. If someone has offended us, especially a close friend or family member, then we owe it to each other as sisters to either pick up the phone and call the offender or visit her in person. Oftentimes, the offender had no idea she had been hurtful! Choosing to unfriend someone without the careful consideration of the full scope of the situation is simply adding fuel to the fire and can make others think of you as immature and untrustworthy. It's hard to be tight friends with a loose cannon.

Choosing to unfriend someone without the careful consideration of the full scope of the situation is simply adding fuel to the fire and can make others think of you as immature and untrustworthy. It's hard to be tight friends with a loose cannon.

On the other hand, when we begin to notice a consistent negative response to a specific person's status updates or we have been repeatedly hurt and offended by her behavior, it might be time to unfriend her. As we have already discussed, we do indeed have a responsibility to guard and protect our hearts. Continually subjecting our hearts to unhealthy behavior requires a boundary, and the boundary is often to either block or unfriend the person who is a threat to our hearts. This should be done with both behavior-grace and forgiveness-grace. Forgive her (don't forget what lack of forgiveness does to you!) speak a blessing over her, and protect your heart. However, if she contacts you and asks why she was removed from your friend list, be prepared to give her a loving and truthful answer. Ignoring her shows disrespect. I realize she might have disrespected you or others in the first place, but as followers of Jesus, we want to choose to take the higher road of not repaying evil with evil (1 Peter 3:9; Romans 12:17). Though our friend might be offensive or hurtful, we are called to be proactive and not reactive. Her sin doesn't give us a free pass to sin, too.

Finally, just as we need to commit to using our spoken words wisely, we also need to make the same promise with our written words as well. During the election season of 2012, I was saddened to see so many personal attacks against both candidates in various Facebook status updates. When we claim to be believers and desire for others to know Jesus, it's very confusing when we publish negative and hateful words toward another person. Though we may not agree with the politics of a particular candidate, we need to be discussing the issues, rather than the person, with behavior-grace. This is another example of the loss of credibility that occurs when we fly off the handle and begin to claim our stance as right in exchange for what is biblically right. When we profess to follow Jesus but our actions don't align, we give the world a glimpse of what's really on our minds.

3. Texting: Have you ever sat down to a much-anticipated dinner with a friend only to spend the evening talking between her incoming text messages and responses? I have been in that situation, and it left me feeling a bit frustrated. I love my friend dearly, but let's face it—in this season of mothering, I don't have a lot of time to get together with my girlfriends. When I do have time with them, it is precious and I want to focus solely on them. If there is a situation in which you might need to text during your time with a friend, explain why you are leaving your phone on the table and only pick it up if that emergency message is received. This might sound inflexible; however, our face-to-face relationships should be the first priority. If you just can't wait until the end of dinner, excuse yourself and go to the restroom to check your messages! However, if this is the case, I do suggest you work through the steps in the P.R.E.S.E.N.T. process.

In the end, technology's good and evil is based upon how we choose to use it. If we are negative, lack behavior-grace, and fail to have boundaries around our technology usage, then technology is going to be an evil. However, if we focus on the positive, handle ourselves with behavior-grace, and integrate boundaries when they are needed, technology is good. Regardless, there is nothing that takes the place of in-real-life friendships, and good, old-fashioned hospitality can help these relationships grow.

DISCUSSION QUESTIONS

1. *In what ways has technology helped your relationships? What ways has it inhibited your relationships?*

2. *Have you ever received a "zinger" e-mail? How did you respond? Would you do it differently today?*

3. *Have you ever been unfriended on Facebook? How did it make you feel? On the other hand, have you ever had to unfriend someone? Why?*

4. *Do you think you need to implement the P.R.E.S.E.N.T. process? If so, which step seems to tackle your greatest area of need?*

5. *Is there someone you can invite to your home this week? Get it scheduled, sister!*

CHAPTER EIGHT

TOMORROW'S HEART SISTERS
Teaching Our Daughters to Be Good Friends

So, mothers, be good to your daughters, too.

John Mayer

I've had many people tell me, "You are so much like your mom!" While it's true we differ in many ways, we are also shockingly similar. Our mannerisms are alike, and our sense of humor tends to be on the same crazy wavelength, too. Hilariously enough, my mother gets a kick out of spending time with my daughter and me because "it's just like watching you grow up all over again!" If I mention Sarah has dug her heels in about something, I'm usually met with a short silence and an ever-so-faint snicker I can hear even though she doesn't think I can. I know what that snicker communicates: been there, done that. With you.

While it's also true there are many women who are nothing like their mothers, one fact remains: girls learn how to navigate relationships by watching how their mothers navigate their own. Like it or not, they're watching. If that makes you a little uneasy in your seat, don't worry—you're not alone. I'm squirming as I write.

While researching for her book *The Twisted Sisterhood*, author Kelly Valen found that 88 percent of the three thousand women she polled believe there is an undercurrent of negativity and meanness within the female culture. Similarly, 84 percent of the same women claim they have suffered "real, genuine wounding at the hands of another woman."[1] My guess is this is not a shocking statistic to you. My other guess is that you can likely personally identify with having been seriously wounded by another female in your life a time or two. You're in good company, sister.

If 88 percent of the female population polled would like to see a change in the culture of women, then it's probably something we all need to stand up and take notice of, don't you think? When my friends and I were discussing this statistic, we were all in agreement that we would like to see more of a sisterhood among women. Yet the question of "how can little old me impact such a massive need?" boiled to the surface. The answer is in equipping our most precious resource of the future: our daughters. Many of you know the "Starfish Story," but in case you don't, I'll offer a quick recap. A man was walking along the shore of the ocean, throwing starfish back into the ocean as they washed up on the sand. A passerby walked by and asked, "Why are you doing this? Look at this beach! You can't save all these starfish. You can't begin to make a difference!" The man was contemplative and after a few moments, he bent down, picked up another starfish, and hurled it as far as he could into the ocean. Then he looked up at the passerby and replied, "Well, I made a difference to that one!" Just like the man who threw the washed-up starfish back into the ocean, we mothers of daughters have the power to guide our girls and show them how to navigate life in the world of women—one girl at a time.

The legacy is ours to leave. Guiding girls to God will place our daughters on the path to finding good girlfriends.

The legacy is ours to leave. Guiding girls to God will place our daughters on the path to finding good girlfriends.

What kind of friends do you want your daughter to have? Do you want her to be with girls who fight with each other and talk behind one another's backs? Or do you want her to spend time with girls who are kind, will say "I'm sorry" when they're wrong, and are genuinely too busy enjoying one another's company to engage in too much drama? I know which one I choose.

The good news is that you can greatly influence the trajectory of your daughter's relationships. While you might hear "girls will be girls" when catty behavior among your daughters and her friends emerge, this doesn't have to be the accepted truth. In fact, I personally believe this attitude is how 88 percent of women came to feel the need for an overhaul in the culture of women. When we make statements like "girls will be girls," we simply sweep the issues they're facing under the rug and evade having to engage in any intentional teaching on how to be a Heart Sister. When we leave children, tweens, teens, and even adults to their own devices without any guidance, the sinful nature of the flesh will take over and if not caught in time, it can be very difficult to reprogram their self-centered way of thinking.

A few months ago, my daughter was exceptionally quiet. My mama-radar began to sound that something was wrong, but I had no idea what it could be. I can usually sense when she's quiet because she's angry versus being quiet because she's sad, and on this particular evening, it was the latter. When I asked what was going on, she said she was told one of her friends, who is two years older, didn't like to play with her anymore because she didn't like Sarah. Sarah still likes to pretend and play make-believe, and her older friend was no longer interested. Of course, this happens with older friends; however, it was the unkind things this girl said about Sarah that stung the most. She was devastated. This was our first voyage on the journey of personal rejection, and it hurt. I know. I've been there on many occasions myself.

Recognizing it was no accident this should emerge while I was writing this particular chapter, I prayed. I've done a lot of praying since becoming a mother, but before I have discussions of this magnitude with my daughter, I pray like crazy because I know it's not me that will teach her. The Holy Spirit is the teacher, but God often uses me to reach her. Here's the thing: my flesh side wanted to give in to the mama bear feelings. I wanted to (1) take the little girl who said those unkind things about my daughter behind our house and let her know what I thought of her, (2) sweep this under the rug as quickly as possible because it was seven thirty in the evening and I was tired, and (3) avoid this conversation because, truth be told, I was terrified I might say something that would crush her further and then she would never want to talk to me about anything ever again.

Thank God for God. Really. A magical thing happened that night in the quiet of that pink and green, horse-decorated bedroom. We talked for an hour and God showed up—big-time. Now before you think, *Well, good for you, Natalie*, let me assure you of this: He'll show up for you, too. Parenting is hard stuff, sisters. We can't do it alone. We need a compass, and God's just waiting to be asked to point us north. So if we want to contribute to lasting positive change in the culture of women, our daughters are our most valuable assets. They're the key to generational change, but how do we teach them to be good friends and encourage other women? We start one day, one moment at a time. We do the right thing, and then we do the next right thing, and we just keep going and we just keep trusting. However, if you need a little help, here's how you can get started:

1. **Learn how to be a healthy friend yourself.** You can't teach something you don't know yourself. Back in the days when I was a teacher, my least favorite subjects were the ones I had absolutely no personal experience with. The same is true for us: we can't teach healthy friendships with the end goal of instructing our daughters how to be Heart Sisters if we haven't learned how to be a Heart Sister ourselves. You are in the process of learning right now because you're reading this book, so kudos to you for taking the initiative to improve your friendships. Be patient with yourself as you reprogram your ways of thinking about women and have the courage to choose relationship over strife. You can do it, sister. For those days when you feel like you can't, perhaps this simple acrostic can help you remember the words to use. We all need to "W.A.T.C.H. I.T.," don't we? Keep in mind, while this is written for our daughters, we can use it as adult women as well.

Welcome others: There's nothing worse than walking into a group of girls and feeling as if you're invisible. If someone walks up to your friends and you, smile at her. If you don't know her, introduce yourself. Ask her to play or just hang out. No one likes the cold shoulder. A welcoming friend is a wonderful friend.

Ask questions: After you have welcomed her, ask her a few questions about who she is. Pull her into what you are talking about. People are God's gift to us, dear daughter. We can learn so much from each other. Make her feel heard by listening well.

Talk with words that build up, not tear down. The old saying about sticks and stones is a lie. Words do hurt. You can choose to build someone up or tear her down just by what you choose to let out of your mouth. When we use our words to tear others down, it's usually because of our own insecurity—the object of our venom is an innocent victim. Not to mention, when we speak ugliness over others, we reveal what's inside our own hearts. On the flip side, when we choose to use words that build up, we encourage each other. We give grace to one another and show others that we are safe, and can be trusted with their hearts. Words can build up or tear down, encourage or discourage, and influence or kill dreams. Choose them well.

Choose friends wisely. This isn't meant to be exclusive—it is not OK to leave someone out because she's not dressed the right way or because she's been labeled as a bit "weird." Choosing friends wisely is about spending time with people who encourage you to love God and be your best self. Unfortunately, there will be girls out there who will not be kind. They will enjoy putting others down, and they'll be your friend one day and your enemy the next. Although we want to pray for these girls and still must handle them with love and grace, we certainly don't have to be their BFF. In fact, there is an old saying that warns us to "be careful of the company you keep." This means if you are spending time with a crowd that bullies others, even if you aren't a bully, you just might be considered one simply because of who you choose to hang around. When you spend time with friends, others assume you enjoy their company. If you enjoy the company of a bully or someone who makes fun of others, then people will believe you do, too. Even if you don't.

Have grace. Your friends will make mistakes. They'll say things that will hurt your feelings and they'll make choices that will sadden you. No one is perfect. And here's the thing: you will need grace from others, too. You have to give grace to get grace. Your friends will need forgiveness-grace, which means they'll need you to forgive them even if they don't seek your forgiveness. However, they will also need behavior-grace. Behavior-grace is the kind of grace we extend simply by showing kindness when we would prefer to not be so kind. It's not retaliating from a hurt with poisonous words. It's remembering we are all in different places in our relationship with God. Grace is an essential piece of a Heart Sister friendship!

Integrate healthy boundaries. While we do need to have grace with others, we also might need to release a relationship if we're repeatedly hurt. An example of this is when a friend threatens to no longer be your friend if you don't do things her way. This is called manipulation, and Heart Sisters don't do that to each other.

Boundaries are also needed if a friend is encouraging you to do what you know is wrong. Heart sisters spur one another on and encourage each other to walk closely with God. Sin separates us from God. If a friend is encouraging you to sin, then she's separating you from God. It's true we all sin. And it's true that God does not have a "severity of sins" scale. All sins are equal in His book. However, if a friend is repeatedly encouraging you to behave inappropriately with boys or drink alcohol or smoke, she doesn't have your best interests at heart. Also, if she is cruel to others and sometimes to you, she doesn't have your best interests at heart. Putting a boundary around the relationship can be done with behavior-grace and forgiveness-grace, and while it might be difficult at times, it will be worth the freedom. We'll talk a bit more about "mean girls" later in this chapter.

Tell the truth but speak it with love. When we lie to each other, we violate trust whether we are caught in our lie or not. If we are trying to be girls of God, we will be less convincing about His truths if we don't value truth in our own relationships. Be a person who values truth, so if you are ever in the position to speak the real Truth, you are trusted. But be careful—you also need to watch how you deliver the truth. There's a difference between being honest and being candid. Being honest is delivering truth for your benefit. It's spouting off things that could be hurtful to another person because "I'm just being honest." However, being candid is sharing truth in a way that is loving and has the other person's best interest at heart. Being honest means I'm all about me, but being candid means I'm all about you. Jesus calls us to put others before us, so when we're candid, we're obeying God.

Let's continue with how to encourage our daughters to have healthy relationships with other girls—girls who eventually become women.

2. Die to self. Yes, yet another area of our lives when we must die to ourselves for the sake of our children. I'm pretty sure this is why God makes us parents: He teaches us so much about His love when we begin this journey of motherhood. Can you imagine if I had gone with the instincts of my flesh in the case of my daughter? I'm afraid I would have taught her to get even, to keep score, and to give in to anger. I would have prioritized my need to defend over the development of her heart. I also would have shown fear to have a tighter grip than truth.

I haven't always followed God's ways in mothering my children. In fact, I have followed my own fleshy ways on many occasions and still do. Which is why I need to rejoice when those effective mothering moments do occur because it's in them when I realize how just much I love being a mother. I know we're all tired. I know there are days when you wish you didn't have to talk so much about every little thing. But trust me—this intentional instruction is teaching your daughter how to win the battle *and* the war. Most of all, you're helping her become a Heart Sister, and by doing this, you are making a generational impact. Power to the mother.

3. Be intentional with talking about your own friendships. My daughter doesn't like when I leave now and then in the evenings, yet it gives us an opportunity to discuss the fact that mom needs time with friends, too. My kids like to lay on the guilt, and admittedly, sometimes I take the bait. Yet when I reverse the situation, it jolts me back to reality: would it be healthy if I made my daughter feel guilty about spending time with her friends? Absolutely not! The same is true of us mamas: it's not healthy when we allow our children to guilt us into not spending time with friends. Spending time with girlfriends is essential to our sanity, and I strongly believe I'm a better mother because of my Heart Sisters.

Likely because this subject is my passion, my daughter and I have great conversations about my friendships, and I'm able to share what I value in a friend as well. We have had discussions about boundaries I have had to put into place in my own friendships, and we've discussed how to still be loving to someone who has hurt your feelings. It's also a good idea to teach our daughters about different kinds of friends, such as the inner, middle, and outer heart friends we discussed in chapter 3. Our daughters model what they see, but they can't always interpret what's going on. They need a little help, and this help comes in the form of intentional conversations.

4. This one is critical: connect with your daughter on the heart level. Your daughter's first Heart Sister is you. This doesn't mean you confuse the line between being her friend and being her mother, but it does mean you check in daily with the state of her heart. It means you listen to her without judgment and are there for her when she needs help with tough social situations. You are her soft place to land even when she feels like the world is against her. We want our daughters to believe we will never turn our backs on them, don't we? Not to mention our children learn about the character of God through our own behavior and He never turns His back on us and cares deeply about the state of our hearts.

In full disclosure, I don't care if my children are the smartest kids in their class. I don't care if they win the science fair, and I don't care if they are the spelling bee champions. However, I do care deeply about the state of their hearts. I care that they are kind to others. I care that they value people over things. I care that they look people in the eye when they're speaking. I care that they embrace truth and defend the weak. Each day, I ask who they play with at recess and who they sit with at lunch. I inquire about kids who might be feeling left out because being the spelling bee champ is a wonderful accomplishment, but it's not going to impact the kingdom of God much. Characteristics of the heart will have a far greater impact on the world.

The best way to connect with your daughter is by keeping the lines of communication open. The best way to keep the lines of communication open is to (1) not allow shock or dis-approval to take over your face when she tells you something, (2) not turn everything into a long, drawn-out lesson, and (3) continuously lead her along the right path by placing situations back in her lap. This means asking guiding questions such as "How did that make you feel?" and sympathizing with phrases such as, "I know it hurts when you feel left out because I've felt left out, too." Shock and disapproval is judgment, and no one likes to feel judged. I know when I feel like I'm being judged, I shut down when I'm around the one doing the judging, and I censor my words. We don't want this to happen with our daughters because, again, we want to be a soft place for them to land. I once heard a wise parenting quote about raising our children: "Listen to your kids when they tell you the little things so one day they will grow up and tell you the big things."

Second to keeping the lines of communication open is spending one-on-one time with your daughter. This doesn't have to be fancy or expensive—it can be as simple as talking in bed at the end of the day. However, it *is* fun to get out and do something together and just have some fun! Dannah Gresh, the creator of a ministry called The Secret Keeper Girl, has created a wonderful book of mother-daughter date ideas titled *8 Great Dates for Moms and Daughters*.[2] While I haven't yet started this with my daughter, I have friends who have used this resource and love its intentional conversation topics and Bible-based teaching of hard topics like boys and purity.

In addition, my own Heart Sister, Erin Bishop, began a ministry called The Whatever Girls based on Philippians 4:8: "Whatever is true, whatever is noble, whatever is right, whatever is pure, whatever is lovely, whatever is admirable—if anything is excellent or praiseworthy—think about such things." The Whatever Girls is intended to be a group of mothers and daughters committed to strengthening their relationships with God, one another, and their peers. The idea is all of the girls and mothers are hearing the same language and living by the same beliefs so the girls will have one another as support and accountability when they are in the world. While several Whatever Girls groups are sprouting up across the country, there is freedom in the structure and content of each group as long as they adhere to the mission of the ministry. Erin's group of mothers and daughters meets at her home every other Tuesday night for fellowship and discussion.[3]

We can be doing all the right things and reading all the right parenting books, but it's an inevitable rite of passage for our daughters: mean girls. There's a lot of buzz these days (pardon the pun) about girls who are Queen Bees, also known as "mean girls." In her book *Queen Bees and Wannabes*, Rosalind Wiseman discusses the social structure that can sometimes emerge among young girls and women. The Queen Bees are the often unkind leaders of a pack of girls who will do whatever it takes to be in control and in charge. The worker bees are the sidekicks to the queen. They also have some power and influence over their peers, but not as much as the queen. The wannabees are the girls who would love to be a queen bee or a worker bee. They will do whatever it takes to gain entry into this "in" crowd and are often the target of bullying. The sting hurts—Queen Bees can make our girls doubt, pout, and feel left out.

While I don't like to place people in categories, I think it's safe to conclude many of us have vacillated among all three of these labels. It's also possible we as mothers have graduated from these stereotypes through maturity and can now consider ourselves Gamma women. A Gamma woman is one who "stands in the center of a web of positive personal connections: she aims to bring out the best in herself and others."[4] According to a study conducted by Meredith, a publisher of more than twenty-one women's magazines, many women in their twenties are more interested in interaction rather than competition through the exchange of ideas, information, and opinions. A Queen Bee model of community is more authoritarian and "my way or the highway" whereas a Gamma style of community is a much more we're-in-this-together type of attitude. Heart Sisters are Gamma girls.

When I started high school back in the late 1980s, I was bullied by girls who were older than me. My hair was quite long then—about halfway down my back. I attracted attention from some of the older boys in my school, and the other girls didn't like that. I didn't even know the girls who decided I was a threat.

As if starting high school wasn't intimidating enough, a pack of two to three girls chose to follow me around the halls during the first two weeks of school with shears they would open and close inches from the back of my head. I can still hear the slicing of those blades to this day. They were determined to scare me

Big mean girls create little mean girls. Those little mean girls then grow up and teach another generation of little mean girls.

by threatening to cut off my long hair right there in front of my English class. I was terrified.

Why do girls do things like this? What would possess a group of girls to select someone they had never even met and follow her around the school with scissors, threatening to cut off her hair?

Remember how we talked about the power of modeling earlier in this chapter? Big mean girls create little mean girls. Those little mean girls then grow up and teach another generation of little mean girls. See how the cycle continues? My family and I love watching old episodes of *Little House on the Prairie*. We are continuously in awe of the cruel antics and words of Nellie Oleson. Is she not just the original mean girl or what? Yet the more episodes we watch, the more sympathetic I feel toward Nellie because it wasn't really her fault she was such a bully. Her mother was a big mean girl who created a little mean girl. Nellie came by her Queen Bee status naturally.

I realize there are situations when a mother does everything right but her daughter is still a mean girl. Hurting people hurt people. Perhaps this girl just found out her parents are divorcing. Or maybe her beloved grandmother passed away and she's angry. Or maybe she is the new girl at school and doesn't want anyone to pity her or tease her so she adopts a tough-girl image. As difficult as this is even for adult women, this is the perfect opportunity to teach our daughters to have compassion for those who are hurting, even though someone is unkind, and pray for our enemies. Matthew 5:43-44 says "You have heard that it was said, 'Love your neighbor and hate your enemy.' But I tell you, love your enemies and pray for those who persecute you." Praying for those who have hard hearts toward you can soften your heart toward them.

Mean girls exist because, quite truthfully, school administrators and teachers are sometimes scared of the mean girls, too. If the Queen Bee is the daughter of a prominent family with a lot of influence, it's possible they won't want to rock the boat by pursuing an end to the behavior. Instead, comments such as "Just ignore them" or "You're overreacting" make victims feel unheard and unprotected. When we fail to pursue an end to this manipulation, we are, in essence, saying we condone what is happening. If we fail to stop the Queen Bee, she will continue to sting.

Understanding that mean girls exist and why they do, what can we, as mothers, do when our daughters inevitably have an experience with a mean girl? Our goal is to create Gamma girls: girls that are able to navigate conflict in a healthy manner and can treat others and themselves kindly even if they feel jealous, angry, or powerless. Gamma girls develop by:

1. **Knowing where they obtain their identity.** When we allow the world to determine our daughters' identities, we teach them they are based on superficial things that could be taken away at any moment. This is a slippery slope of insecurity that encourages our girls to always be searching for something of the world to fill that God-shaped hole. When we teach our girls who they are in His eyes, and not the world's eyes, we are encouraging them to anchor in some pretty deep roots that won't be able to be shaken by the insults of mean girls—or anyone else for that matter.

2. **Having a mother who talks through the hard stuff without judgment or criticism.** Children are keen observers and lousy

interpreters. They often need help with interpreting the reality of frustrating and scary situations. When we show our daughters we care by listening to their hearts and helping them find a healthy solution, we confirm what a Heart Sister truly is. We show them we are safe, and our lack of judgment and criticism ensures they will talk to us again when they need help.

As you are discussing tough situations with your daughter, I want to caution you about one thing: be careful not to promise you won't talk to anyone about what is happening. If she asks you to not tell anyone, you can simply answer with "I can't make that promise because if someone is in danger, I have a responsibility to help and let the parents know what is going on." I would encourage you to guide your daughter to the same conclusion, so she won't be hesitant to talk to you about tough stuff in the future. She needs to know you will be talking appropriately to parents or teachers because doing this behind her back without her knowledge would betray a confidence between your daughter and you. It's a delicate balance between being a person of safety for our daughters yet remaining an adult who serves to protect and care for other children as well.

3. **Talking through a plan of what to do when a mean girl attacks.** After the first month of high school, I broke down and told my mother what was happening with the girls who followed me with scissors. Of course, she was saddened to hear I had been experiencing this at school for a month, but she listened without a shocked look on her face and didn't interrupt or try to fix things right away. Though I now know her inner mama bear was raging within, she patiently talked through our options of what to do when the mean girls struck again. I remember feeling a sense of peace in knowing I had an adult on my side, and I also felt

very grown-up that we were going to try to solve this problem together first before going to the administrators of the school.

Though I wanted to turn around, grab those scissors, and gouge out the eyeballs of my perpetrators, my mother encouraged me to choose another method (thankfully): "Smile at them. Say hello. Most of all, don't retaliate or explode because that's exactly what they want. If it gets too big to handle, go to a trusted teacher. If a trusted teacher doesn't exist, go to an administrator. If no one is doing anything to help you, call me."

4. **Knowing when it's time to talk to school personnel or parents.** Eventually, my mother had to meet with the administrators of my school, as the mean girls didn't stop with the scissors. We tried to handle the situation on our own first, but our plan didn't work so well—I continued to be followed and threatened. Luckily, after this meeting, the girls stopped, and I began to feel like I could breathe again while I was at school. My grades improved, and I had far less anxiety when I wasn't worrying about when I would next find scissors near my ear. My mother was my advocate, and I discovered I could trust her to protect me even when she wasn't with me.

Our girls need us. Even when they don't want to admit they need us, they need us. Even when they roll their eyes and act like we don't know anything about anything, they need us. Our daughters learn so much about relationships from watching our own, and they need help with the tough relational situations they will encounter. They need us to be the Heart Mothers God created us to be. Our girls need us to be the women from Titus 2:4 who teach the younger generation how to navigate in the world. They need us to rise up and be the change we want to see in the culture of women: one girl at a time.

DISCUSSION QUESTIONS

1. *What kind of friends do you want your daughter to have?*

2. *What do you want your daughter to know about healthy friendship?*

3. *Which part of the W.A.T.C.H. I.T. acronym is the biggest challenge for you? Why?*

4. *Have you ever had an experience with a Queen Bee? Were you ever a Queen Bee, a Worker Bee, or a Wannabee?*

5. *How can you connect with your daughter on a heart level? Do you know what communicates love to her?*

CHAPTER NINE

HEART SISTERS AT THE OFFICE OR MINISTRY TEAM

If you just set out to be liked, you would be prepared to compromise on anything at any time and you would achieve nothing.

—Margaret Thatcher

I had no idea I was about to step into a hornet's nest when I took the reins of a women's ministry a few years ago. Since I didn't become a true believer until I was twenty-seven years old, I believed that everyone who served together in ministry wore rose-colored glasses and talked about rainbows and unicorns all day. I was wrong.

Each of us, believer or nonbeliever, is disabled by the flesh. We don't receive the holy grail of perfection after we accept Jesus—just His grace for the myriad of occasions when we'll need it. As a woman in leadership, you will need a whole lot of grace—the best leaders are those who make mistakes and learn from them.

When you make the decision to follow Jesus, you are bestowed with an invisible target mounted to your chest. The more you do for the kingdom, the more the target grows. If your target remains small, you aren't much of a threat. But the bigger your target, the more of a threat you become to the enemy. I am not one to look for Satan under every rock nor do I ever want to glorify his power in any way; however, spiritual warfare is real and it happens frequently to those who are doing much to expand the kingdom of God. Those with big targets are doing big things for God, and this doesn't make Satan very happy.

When your target increases in size, be prepared for stuff to happen that you may not have seen coming. Before you read these various scenarios, let me reassure and encourage you by saying my experience as the leader of a women's ministry group was among the top five personal growth experiences I've had in my life. While I still have much to learn, I am far wiser now than I was before. It's kind of like wishing we could go back to high school with the knowledge we have now and do it all over again. What I have learned as a leader is not meant to discourage you but rather to equip you so when situations arise, you won't feel so completely alone or wonder if you are doing a good job and for crying out loud, should you step down? No, sister. Forge ahead. You're in good company—let's not forget there were some pretty notable people from the Bible who were called into leadership as well and their path wasn't always so easy, either.

David was appointed to be the next king following Saul at a very young age. In fact, he was just a young, small shepherd when God called him into ministry. Saul was supposed to have been his mentor, but Saul eventually turned against his own protégé. When Saul refused to obey God after he was asked to destroy all of the Amalekites and their possessions, he lost God's favor. The successor to the throne, young David, was then given this coveted favor, and Saul wasn't so happy. To add fuel to the fire, when David defeated Goliath, Jewish women celebrated in the streets by chanting, "Saul has slain his thousands, and David his tens of thousands!" (1 Samuel 18:7). Not surprisingly, this didn't go over so well with King Saul. He made it his personal mission to destroy David, and he literally chased the successor to the throne through the mountains and valleys of their land for twenty years.

There is much leaders can glean from this story. Instead of focusing on improving the kingdom and working for the betterment of the people in his jurisdiction, the primary focus of Saul's reign became seeking his own revenge against David. Saul allowed jealousy, bitterness, and anger to thwart his energy because his own ego was far more important than the people he was serving. To his credit, David did not retaliate in negativity but instead, kept his eyes focused upon God and His will. In fact, most of the Psalms were written from various caves and other outdoor dwellings David was forced to hide in while being pursued by Saul. It wasn't an easy time, yet David continued to choose peace. In fact, when given the opportunity to kill Saul while he slept in a cave, David declined.

We are told in Proverbs 16:18 that pride comes before a fall and, eventually, Saul succumbed to his pride. He tragically committed suicide after losing a battle with the Philistines—he fell hard. I know you are thanking me for such an uplifting story, but there is a point in the telling of this sad tale. The moral of the

We all make mistakes, but it's what we do with those mistakes that matters most.

story is to search our motives before we choose to accept a position of leadership.

When we step into leadership positions, it's critical we examine our own hearts and ask ourselves three questions:

1. Am I accepting this position because I desire recognition and like to be in control and have power?

2. Am I accepting this position in humility and will be open to being molded during this process?

3. Do I possess a passion for this ministry?

If you are following in the footsteps of Saul, then fame and power might be your goal. On the other hand, if you have a genuine passion for the ministry and, in humility, accept and understand this will be an experience for growth, then you are likely going to be much like David's style of leadership. We all make mistakes, but it's what we do with those mistakes that matters most.

While we are on the topic of making mistakes, let's talk about the inevitable: your critics. Just as you are guaranteed to make mistakes, I can assure you there will also be critics. While we can't negate our responsibility, it's wise to follow the P.E.G. System found in chapter 5 when this happens because if you are a humble leader, more often than not your critics' complaints are more about them than they are about you. This doesn't mean you can dismiss every rebuke or complaint and negate responsibility. If you have worked through the P.E.G. System and don't feel like you have done anything wrong, then it's very likely the person who is complaining is simply committed to misunderstanding you. Bless her, forgive her, and move on, sister.

A funny thing happens when you become a leader in a ministry or at the office. Because of your position, if you say something foolish or have a lapse in judgment, you can so easily be labeled as an imposter or someone who is not walking the talk. Just because you are promoted to a position of leadership, it doesn't mean you've been promoted to perfection. You are just as human as you were before—in fact, you will often find yourself in stickier situations because of your position, so there's certainly more room for mistakes to be made. However, those very mistakes can build your wisdom and experience and make you an even more effective leader.

If you are accused of not walking the talk, let me reassure you, you're in good company. In fact, Paul alludes to this in his letters to the Romans when he admits,

> So the trouble is not with the law, for it is spiritual and good. The trouble is with me, for I am all too human, a slave to sin. I don't really understand myself, for I want to do what is right, but I don't do it. Instead, I do what I hate. But if I know that what I am doing is wrong, this shows that I agree that the law is good. So I am not the one doing wrong; it is sin living in me that does it. And I know that nothing good lives in me, that is, in my sinful nature. I want to do what is right, but I can't. I want to do what is good, but I don't. I don't want to do what is wrong, but I do it anyway. But if I do what I don't want to do, I am not really the one doing wrong; it is sin living in me that does it. (Romans 7:14-20 NLT)

Some will want you to make everyone happy all the time, but then you only have to remember Margaret Thatcher's quote about pleasing everyone to remember what happens to those who do. If you allow your critics to uproot you every time they have a complaint, you will no longer be anchored to the soil of your beliefs and you'll sway with the wind.

Loud voices will often drown out the ones who are not. They're also rarely indicative of the feelings of the majority, too. Sure, there are times when protesting a social issue is defending the weak and oppressed, but that's not what I'm talking about here. I'm talking about those who have a personal agenda against your success and are threatened by your position of leadership or your job. I ran across a quote on Pinterest the other day that read, "Never waste your time trying to explain who you are to people who are committed to misunderstanding you." If someone is committed to misunderstanding you, then she's just waiting for you to stumble, and when you do, she will pounce. I would have saved myself from a whole lot of stress if I had just known I won't, and can't, please everyone.

In those moments when you feel like David being pursued by Saul, read Psalm 62—over and over again if you must. Your hope and honor comes from *Him*—not *them*. Ironically, this is a Psalm written by David when Saul was hot on his trail! I'm pretty sure God is telling leaders to expect persecution—it's part of the job. But there is also a time to be pruned and a time to bear fruit. If you are experiencing a tough season of pruning, there will be a day when you will bear fruit, and this fruit will be in the form of knowledge and wisdom.

So if I haven't thoroughly scared you away from leadership, are you ready to jump into the saddle? You can do it, friend. But remember this: the ministry you are leading is directly impacted by the health of your leadership team. Leadership has a trickle-down effect. If you are committed to obedience to God, then your mission will bloom, but if you are backbiting and untrustworthy, your mission will die on the vine.

As with any healthy relationship, humility is critical to your success as a leader. You *will* make mistakes. You are learning this route, and in the process of learning, mistakes are aplenty. Again, it's not the mistakes that matter; it's what you do *after* the mistakes.

A friend of mine confided in me she once experienced a verbal backlash from two women in front of her ministry team several years ago. Her team was watching, and she possessed enough self-control to not fight back though her flesh tempted her to do so. While it was incredibly difficult, she chose what was right rather than what she desired. She retreated from the scene to pray and seek God's direction and by the next morning, she felt convicted to go to the two women and apologize for her role in hurting them. Truthfully, I didn't understand what my friend did wrong, but her humility was a beautiful example of servant leadership for the women on her team.

When apologizing for our role in someone else's hurt, we aren't admitting fault; instead, we are recognizing we played some kind of a role in her pain—intentionally or not. This is precisely what my friend did. She obeyed God and modeled grace and humility to a team of twelve women watching her response. Knowing the women on her ministry team, I asked one of them what she thought of the way the situation was handled. "It gave me even more confidence in the leadership of this ministry!" she said. Our actions matter—big-time. Titus 2:7-8 says, "In

When hearts invest in a mission, the return is always profitable.

everything set them an example by doing what is good. In your teaching show integrity, seriousness and soundness of speech that cannot be condemned, so that those who oppose you may be ashamed because they have nothing bad to say about us." Amen. Literally.

We also want to strive to be humble in our authority. I have seen the most unlikely of people become authoritarian when stepping into a leadership role. If you begin with an "I'm in charge" attitude, your team or coworkers will feel as though their input won't make a difference and will withdraw. I don't want to lead a team of puppets—even if the puppets are politely disagreeing with me! If your team doesn't feel some kind of ownership in the ministry or company, then they will likely not connect with its mission on the heart level. We want everyone to connect to the ministry on the heart level, because this is when the best work for the ministry's development can be done. When hearts invest in a mission, the return is always profitable.

Last winter, I had the pleasure of attending a conference sponsored by Proverbs 31, a women's ministry led by writer and speaker Lysa TerKeurst. During one of her sessions, she described three ways to deliver a message. First, you could deliver your message from a platform in which you speak down to those hearing your message. This is the "I have all of the answers" approach, and its effectiveness isn't so strong. Next, you could tone it down a little and deliver your message from the front door. You're still expressing your great wisdom but you are likely not as bold as those who choose platform delivery. Finally, you could deliver a message as though you are "in the field," working alongside your listener. Leaders should be "in the field" with a delicate balance of wisdom that can teach and move people while still admitting we don't know it all and are learning just like everybody else. It's the proper ratio of wisdom and humility that makes an effective leader.

When you accept an invitation to lead a ministry or a new position at work, you are not only the leader but the teacher as well. The leadership team of your ministry sets its relational thermostat to the temperature you establish. James tells us that teachers will be judged more harshly than others (James 3:10). Now before you wave the white flag of surrender, let me reassure you of this: if you stay tethered to the truth, you will have no problem. It's when you break away from the tether that you get into the danger of teaching false gospel, which is what James is warning us about.

It's also wise to begin your new position with discussing the team's conflict management plan. God creates everyone to be unique—with unique ways of learning, communicating, and listening. These differences enrich a team working toward a common goal, but they can also lead to conflict. Healthy leadership teams talk about how to walk through conflict in a way that honors God before the conflict arises because proactive thinking fosters a healthy team. Reactive thinking leaves everyone at the mercy of situations and moods and leads to an "anything goes" way of operating that isn't all too healthy for the group. Tools such as the Heart Sisters Agreement found at my blog are helpful because it allows for everyone to know expectations (www.nataliesnapp.com).

If you are leading a women's team of a ministry or are a leader in the workplace, good for you! Your commitment and willingness to use your gifts to serve are undoubtedly blessing many. Though there are moments in which you will be refined, you will emerge with more wisdom and a closer relationship with God. If we humble ourselves to Him, He will equip us. You *will* make mistakes. Have grace with your team, but most of all, have grace with yourself. Remember David? To this day, he is still considered one of the greatest leaders of all time, and he made many mistakes! David admitted his sin, sought forgiveness, and repented, so God shaped him into a respected leader who left a strong legacy of scripture that impacts us even today. You've got this.

DISCUSSION QUESTIONS

1. *What are the qualities of a good leader?*

2. *Think of the life of David. What were his strengths? What were his weaknesses? How did God use him?*

3. *Brainstorm ways you can start your leadership team off on the right foot. What are the team's strengths? Weaknesses?*

4. *How do you react to your critics? What do you think God wants you to learn from them?*

5. *Take a moment to dream: what do you desire for the ministry or company you serve? How can you make that happen?*

CHAPTER TEN

WHAT DOES A HEART SISTER NOT DO?

A doubtful friend is worse than a certain enemy. Let a man be one thing or the other, and we then know how to meet him.

—Aesop, *Aesop's Fables*

We've all heard the phrases about friends and enemies—"With friends like these, who needs enemies?" and "Keep your friends close and your enemies even closer," to name a few. There's even now a term for the friend who also moonlights as your enemy: she's your "frenemy." Sadly enough, I don't think there are many women out there who have never been hurt by another woman.

Before we learn about what makes a Heart Sister, we need to be aware of what a Heart Sister does *not* do. Yet as you read this chapter, please remember there is no condemnation in Jesus. Have grace with yourself. There isn't a person alive who hasn't done at least one of these—in fact, if you're like me, you've done them all. Our mistakes don't define our identity, and people can, and do, change. Remember: it's what we do after we make our mistakes that matters most. If we are humble and can admit when we are wrong, then we are certainly not considered bad friends. Everyone screws up now and then and no one wants to have to keep being reminded of their lack of judgment. God will mold us through our missteps and guide us to good.

In addition, I want to encourage you to not only have grace with yourself but with others as well. Just because you might have a friend who has done a few things we are about to discuss, it doesn't mean she should immediately be dismissed from your life. Just as you are still learning and will make mistakes, so will your friends. God looks at the heart and so should we. The condition of your heart and your friend's heart will determine if she is indeed a Heart Sister. If she is humble, willing to examine her role in a misstep, and conscientious of your feelings, then she is certainly a good friend who just made a mistake. When friends make mistakes, it's not automatic grounds for dismissal.

On the other hand, you might read through this chapter and realize you have been mistreated by another person and either didn't realize it was happening or were too scared to do any-thing about it. If this is the case with you, I would encourage you to pray about establishing healthy boundaries so, above all else, you can protect your heart. There have been moments in my own life when I've realized the very relationships I thought were building me up were actually tearing me down.

Friends are meant to enhance our lives and we are meant to reciprocate. We are to support one another, listen to one another, and of course, laugh with one another! However, less-than-encouraging friendships can actually hinder our relationship with God and, in turn, with others as well. The following actions are what a Heart Sister doesn't do:

I might have ugly heart moments but I don't want those moments to gain momentum and form a heart that's permanently ugly.

1. **A Heart Sister does not gossip.** OK, I realize there is likely not a woman on the planet who has never gossiped. We've all fallen victim to this; in fact, this is the one I struggle with the most. However, I don't really think many of us gossip out of a malicious heart—I think we gossip out of a curious heart. We naturally just want to know about the lives of others, don't we? Why do you think *People* magazine and *Us Weekly* sell so well? We are innately interested in the lives of others.

This being said, gossip is gossip, regardless if it comes from a malicious heart or a curious heart. If we choose to gossip with our friends, we are engaging in behavior that is negative and can tear others down rather than build them up. As followers of Jesus, we want to breathe words that give life, right? We are reminded of this in Proverbs 16:28 as well: "A perverse person stirs up conflict, and a gossip separates close friends." And how about this verse from Proverbs 20:19: "A gossip betrays a confidence; so avoid anyone who talks too much"?

When I'm in the presence of someone who is blatantly cutting down someone else, I immediately think (1) there is something within her own heart that still needs healing, (2) she might be jealous or threatened by this person in some way, (3) there is probably more to this story, and (4) if she is speaking this way about someone else, I might be the next victim. Ugly words expose an ugly heart. In his talk "Overcoming Negativity," Graham Cooke talks about how our words make what is invisible (what's inside us) visible.[1] What do we want people to see? I might have ugly heart moments but I don't want those moments to gain momentum and form a heart that's permanently ugly. The difference is that there is room for grace when our hearts have ugly moments. On the other hand, someone with an ugly heart is certainly one who needs our prayers, but we might also need to establish some boundaries around this relationship as well.

If you are in the presence of others who are gossiping, the most effective way to end the slam session is to refuse to add wood to the fire. Proverbs 26:20 says, "Without wood a fire goes out; without a gossip a quarrel dies down." Silence can verbalize what ten thousand words cannot. Yet at the same time, if you feel compelled to speak against gossip, you can say something along the lines of "I'm really trying to search for the good in us all because I know I need a lot of grace, too." Finally, if the gossip persists, you might want to choose this particular moment to find something that needs your attention so you can leave the room. If gossip is the norm for a group of friends, it might be time to reassess your friends.

2. **A Heart Sister does not use words irresponsibly.** All right, this is another tough one. Since we are all indeed disabled by the flesh, it's a safe assumption to conclude we will say things now and then that don't accurately portray the status of our hearts. We will have moments of open mouth, insert foot. But let me remind us it's what we do *after* that matters! My Heart Sisters and I have laughed on many occasions because one of us will go back to the other to clarify meaning of something said that might have sounded one way, only to find the listener didn't

hear her words negatively at all. Regardless, it's best to cover your bases because there have been occasions when there was indeed hurt, and it's best to err on the side of caution.

We also want to consistently check that our words match our intentions and we are able to stand behind them. If I say I am going to do something, I want to be able to do it! If our lips promise one thing and we consistently do another, our words will become just that: words. In our modern culture, people have become really good at deciphering lip service versus authenticity because we've had to become wise consumers. We now possess an unspoken, invisible meter that tells us when something might be a little, well . . . off. After someone has been burned a few times by what you have said, your words will lose the authority they might have once had—even if you have a strong message.

Finally, resist the urge to use your words to commit to things you know you won't be able to fulfill. This is setting yourself up for failure, and oftentimes, we do this out of our own pride or sense of guilt. In my own experience, I have been unable to stand behind my words at times because I've used my words to overschedule myself. When we are spread too thin, we don't give ourselves enough margin to be able to do what we say we are going to do because we're too busy running around in the barnyard without a head.

3. A Heart Sister is not honest. This sounds weird, doesn't it? In his book *Grace-Based Parenting*, Tim Kimmel explains the difference between being honest and being candid.[2] When we are honest with someone, oftentimes we are sharing for our own benefit rather than for the benefit of the listener. However, if we are candid, we are lovingly sharing for the benefit of the

If you don't want your friend to be on the defense, you have to play the offense with candid love.

listener. Big difference. Once again, it's the heart that determines the temperature in this situation. I can think of many times in which I've said "I'm just being honest!" after I've set free a slew of negativity from my lips. It's true: I was being honest, but it benefitted me and no else. Honesty is no longer my goal: I strive to be candid.

When we are candid, we are thinking of the thoughts and feelings of our friend rather than our own insecurities or agenda. There are moments in which we feel led to speak into something happening in a friend's life—perhaps we need to flip on the light switch for her. The best way to do this is to let her know how much you love her, how much you care about her well-being, and how you are for her, not against her.

At the same time, I have been the one to go to a friend in honesty only to have it backfire horribly. Why? Because what I was sharing with her was for my benefit rather than her own. I was not being candid. My heart was focused upon my own selfish desires and needs, and it put my friend on the defensive. Nothing closes the ears to a seemingly well-intentioned message quicker than an accusatory or combative tone. If you don't want your friend to be on the defense, you have to play the offense with candid love.

4. **A Heart Sister does not stir up conflict.** Haven't we all known someone who loves to stir the pot? Someone who likes to add a pinch or a cup of drama to shake things up a bit? Proverbs 6 warns us against such people:

> *There are six things the Lord hates,*
>   *seven that are detestable to him:*
>   *haughty eyes,*
>   *a lying tongue,*
>   *hands that shed innocent blood,*
>   *a heart that devises wicked schemes,*
>   *feet that are quick to rush into evil,*
>   *a false witness who pours out lies*
>   *and a [person] who stirs up dissension [in the*
> *community] (16-19, emphasis mine)*

The seventh thing listed is those who stir up conflict in the community. The other six things the Lord hates with a righteous hate. However, the seventh thing is what He detests. Now, I don't know about you, but I think the word *detests* is a much stronger word than *hate*. Oftentimes, the person who is stirring up conflict is wounded and suffering horribly in her own captivity. She chooses to stir up conflict because she is suffering so much she either knowingly or unknowingly wants others to suffer as well. Remember the whole "misery loves company" thing? Unfortunately, there is some truth to this warning. However, allow me to throw up the caution flag: you don't have to be their company.

In my own experience, when I notice a consistent pattern of someone stirring up conflict, my safety radar begins to sound. First, I know this person isn't ready to be in a Heart Sister friendship because her emotional maturity is not developed enough to authentically and safely engage with another person's heart. Second, we want to surround ourselves with peacemakers. Sometimes this means speaking up when there's an elephant in the room. Sometimes this means speaking truth against false conflict that is being stirred up. Sometimes it means going to someone for a candid conversation even when it's uncomfortable. A friend who stirs up conflict is not a peacemaker—she's a peace taker.

Isn't there enough taking away from our peace without having help from our friends? We can pray for our sister who is stirring up conflict, and we can even continue to spend time with her. Be wise and steer her to a path of truth and love when you notice the dissension brew starting to percolate. When she feels secure, she will likely no longer have a need to stir up conflict, and your problem is solved! If she remains a peace taker, it might be time for some loving boundaries.

5. A Heart Sister doesn't give her opinion without being asked for it. There are many moments in which we simply want someone to listen to us. We want to know our friend has listened and has heard what is in our hearts. In fact, this is a common complaint in marriage: I don't want him to fix the problem for me: I just want him to listen!

Of course, there are times when a friend doesn't ask but you suspect she might be wanting some direction. Ask her if she would like some help, and if she says yes, go right ahead and candidly share your thoughts!

6. A Heart Sister doesn't criticize your family—particularly your significant other. Yes, there are moments when we need to talk to someone about frustrations in our marriage. No, marriage is not easy (not in my experience at least). However, a Heart Sister will remind you of truth and encourage you to stay in the game and to keep choosing family—there will be better times ahead. All marriages go through valleys, and when my husband and I have experienced them, it's my Heart Sisters who've encouraged me to keep going. Marriage is challenging enough without our friends joining in! However, there are indeed situations in which a spouse is abusive, be it emotionally, physically, or spiritually. Heart Sisters will lovingly speak truth without railing against him and help you get the help you need.

A good friend will also not criticize your children. Again, there might be times when your child is in need of some discipline, but Heart Sisters understand this doesn't define his or her identity—or yours. Like us, our children will make mistakes, too. In fact, we want them to because there is no better teacher than our own mistakes. I would much rather my three make as many mistakes as they possibly can while they're under my roof, so Jason and I can readily be there to steer them toward God and help them pick up the pieces. Our Heart Sisters are on our team and will always root for the success of our marriage and our children.

7. **A Heart Sister listens more than she talks.** I love to talk. While I do consider myself an ambivert, listening more than talking is a tough one for me because I'm an external processor and genuinely love to learn from others through conversation. On the other hand, I once was friends with a woman who constantly talked about herself—and for a very long time. I began to avoid her calls because I knew I didn't have an hour to spend on the phone hearing about her, her, and her. Very rarely did she ask or listen to what was happening in my life. Soon our friendship became a one-way street, and we lost contact because I lacked the energy to keep the relationship going. Which leads us to . . .

8. **A Heart Sister doesn't always turn the conversation back to her.** Friendship is a mutual exchange. It's a give and take and involves asking about the other person. A girlfriend doesn't exist only for our own benefit—we exist for her benefit as well! Heart Sisters enhance one another's lives, and this can't be

done if we don't know what's happening with each other. We find out what's happening with each other through conversation, and conversation is a two-way street.

One of my friends has another friend who only talks about herself and never asks about my friend's life. My friend happens to be a blogger, and after reading about several life experiences on her blog, her friend called her and demanded, "Why didn't you ever tell me about this?" My friend handled it with grace, but the reason she had never told her what was happening? She was never given the opportunity to tell her what was happening.

We all have our moments—it's true we'll have times we need to talk through stuff going on in our lives and the conversation *will* be about us. This is different. When we expect our friendships to always be about us, we become takers who take and take and take but never give.

9. A Heart Sister doesn't boast. Sure, we want to celebrate the good in each other's lives. But there's a difference between celebrating the good and always feeling the need to tell everyone how wonderful we are or our children are or how much money we have or how fast we completed the latest 5k. When someone is boasting, it usually means her ego is so fragile she needs validation from others. She certainly needs our love, and we can encourage her through a generic "That's great!"

When someone brags or boasts, it's often because she's bought into the performance-based concept that doing things, particularly doing things well, buys her love and acceptance. If we can see the boasters in our lives through this lens, our hearts tend to soften. Through our own prayer and the seeds we plant, perhaps she will begin to base her identity on who God says she is instead of what she does.

10. A Heart Sister doesn't make you feel horrible when you spend time with her. Here's a question to ask yourself: how do I usually feel when I leave the presence of my friend? Am I lifted up and encouraged, or do I feel insecure and depressed? How you feel after you spend time with a friend is a good indicator of the effect she has on your mental health. Again, we are meant to sharpen one another. We are meant to enhance one another's lives. And we are meant to encourage, equip, and love. However, it is also true that life can be difficult. There might be times when your friend is experiencing a really hard season of life and needs you to be there.

My friend Jocelyn recently had a close friend who was going through a hard time. She was struggling with a lot of things, including the temptation to make some pretty bad choices. "To be honest, it was exhausting to be her friend during this season. We were longtime friends, and I was the only person who knew what she was facing," Jocelyn said. "She is much better now, but I don't know what would have happened if I had not been faithful even though it was really hard and really draining. It's not that she was a bad, hateful person, but she was lost and I held on to her until she could begin to walk on her own again. Sometimes we can only encourage, equip, and love in one direction for a season."

We are not meant to tear each other down. Nor are we meant to compare or be the victims of covert aggressive, emotional games because . . .

11. A Heart Sister doesn't play emotional games. Among tweens and teens, this is called "emotional bullying." However, I've seen some emotional bullying going on in the realm of adults that would make the hair on the back of your neck stand up. Have you ever realized after two minutes into a conversation you've been sucker-punched? While I once believed this was called passive aggression, I recently learned it's actually considered covert aggression.

The person who is covertly aggressive will often be seen as incredibly charming and warm on the outside but really has an agenda or anger festering on the inside. The covertly aggressive personality knows your own vulnerabilities and will exploit them to either feel better about herself or to get you to do something in her favor. She is very adept at cloaking her feelings and expectations, which is why it's so confusing when we find ourselves a victim of this kind of aggression. Oftentimes, the covertly aggressive personality is unable to take responsibility for her behavior. She is very good at spinning any concerns you might discuss with her so that you leave the conversation feeling as though *you* are the one who has done something wrong.

Emotional manipulation is alive and kicking in the culture of women. However, when we recognize it's happening and know what we can do to protect ourselves, then we are one step closer to making a positive change in the female culture. So how do we handle a friend who is covertly aggressive? We recognize it is happening, and we don't give her what she wants: the authority to name who we are or the power to manipulate us to do what she wants us to do. Though it sounds simple, I know it's not because I've been the victim of covert aggressive personality types more often than I can count. The more you are exposed to this type of manipulation, the better you become at recognizing it when it occurs. Recognition is half the battle. When you refuse to be a pawn in the covert aggressive's game, she will eventually move on and try to checkmate someone else. And we'll pray for them both.

12. A Heart Sister doesn't withhold forgiveness or lack humility. Earlier, I told you about a friend of mine who refused to talk

about a conflict that had transpired between us. She preferred to just sweep it under the rug and pretend it never happened. There was once a time when I would have gone along with that, but I can't agree to it anymore because I know it would impact our relationship. When I expressed this to her, she chose to end our friendship instead of talking through it. When we choose relationship, God is pleased. When we choose strife, Satan is pleased.

Hear me on this, sister: you do not need to stand in the chasm of someone else's unforgiveness. Her inability to forgive doesn't have the power to hold you captive. In chapter 5, we discussed that forgiveness is for you—not necessarily for the one who has hurt you. Remember: it takes one to forgive but two to reconcile. You may never fully reconcile but you can choose to forgive with or without the other person's consent.

But I have to say . . . if someone refuses to forgive or even attempt reconciliation, this equates to covert aggression in my book. If you have experienced a conflict with someone and she seeks to reconcile, you certainly have a choice to reconcile or not. But if you refuse to at least *attempt* reconciliation, you are working against God's will. God is always *for* relationship—with Him and with others, particularly among His believers. Oftentimes, what holds us back from seeking reconciliation is our own pride and fear, and this is a lack of humility.

13. A Heart Sister does not betray a confidence. We are only as good as our word, sisters. Trust is a huge piece of friendship. If we share something we are asked not to share, then we are not standing by our word and honoring our friend. If we are asked not to share something with anyone else, then we probably shouldn't tell anyone. It's that simple. The biggest destroyer of trust between two friends is lack of humility, but a close second is when a friend betrays a confidence. As we've discussed before, if we are going to allow our friends past our front porch and reveal the deepest, ugliest parts of ourselves, then we need to be able to feel the freedom to let our freak flags fly without the threat of broadcast. A true Heart Sister takes that personal stuff and files it away, not sharing it with anyone. This communicates safety and encourages us to continue to be genuine and candid. I've spoken to so many women who have been wounded by women who have shared information they shouldn't have shared with others. Sometimes, it can take the person being betrayed a while to feel like she can trust again. I don't know about you, but I don't want that on my conscience when I lie down for bed each night.

14. A Heart Sister does not abuse boundaries. We are quite busy these days, aren't we? Some of us work outside of the home then work inside the home after hours. Some of us work inside the home all day. There are dishes to unload, meetings to attend, family to visit, spouses who need our attention, and kids who need their mama. One of the most critical needs we possess as women? Rest. We need rest. It's not a sign of weakness to admit we are tired. It's a sign of strength.

I think we could start a revolution among women if we commit to encouraging each other to say no. Not to everything, of course. We can say yes to our families and the areas where we know beyond a shadow of a doubt the Holy Spirit has called us to serve. But if you are overscheduled and tired and you tell me you can't come hear me speak or read my book right at this moment, you will get a resounding "Good for you!" from me. You know why? Because I was once so terribly horrible at this it almost cost me my marriage.

Before I had healthy boundaries, I was burning my candle at both ends, and everyone—my husband, children, friends, and I—was paying for it. Praise be to God for my Heart Sister, Katrina, who stepped in and began to guard my schedule with a fierceness that scared the pants off of me. For at least a month, I pretty much had to clear my schedule with her. It was as if I were an addict in recovery, and in some ways, I was. I was addicted to activity, and I needed to go to rehab.

But you know what started to happen when I surrendered my busy life? I began to learn about the concept of margin. Margin is when we have enough space between activities to decompress. Margin allows us to arrive at places on time, and it gives us space to breathe and enjoy the world around us instead of flitting from one activity to another.

So when a friend says no, will you join me in applauding her? Her no might be at your expense, but remember: she's trying to be proactive and prevent family stress, so be the Heart Sister who encourages her to look out for herself.

This might be a tough chapter to read because all of us have violated at least one of the items on the list of "Heart Sisters Don't." If you're like me, you're guilty of violating all of them. I told you I've carried the cat by the tail, right? If you are hearing a voice telling you that you aren't a very good friend, it's not from God. You may have made mistakes in the past, but today is a new day with new mercies. Yet I believe we become our better selves by examining our not-so-great selves and identifying our own junk that holds us back from healthy relationships. All of these "don'ts" have led to my own personal observations of what a Heart Sister *does*.

DISCUSSION QUESTIONS

1. Is having grace for yourself easy or difficult for you? Why or why not?

2. How do you feel when you are in the presence of someone who is speaking negatively about someone else? What does this tell you about the state of her heart?

3. Discuss the difference between honesty and being candid.

4. Brainstorm how to handle people who stir up dissension. Is there a way to safely encourage them so they don't feel the need to stir the pot?

5. Assess your own commitments. Is there enough margin in your life? If not, are there commitments you can remove so margin can exist?

CHAPTER ELEVEN

WHAT DOES A HEART SISTER DO?

Piglet sidled up to Pooh from behind. "Pooh?" he whispered.
"Yes, Piglet?"
"Nothing," said Piglet, taking Pooh's hand. "I just wanted to be sure of you."

—A. A. Milne

The best is yet to come: sometimes I think we need to examine what something *isn't* before we fully understand what something *is*. Relationships can often be clouded with our own sin as well as the sin of others, and when we mix all of that together, we get a cocktail that can leave us feeling confused. My prayer for you is that by reading what friendship *isn't* in the previous chapter, you will be able to identify what a healthy friendship really *is*.

So now that we know what a Heart Sister doesn't do, what does a Heart Sister do? This is the fun part. It's time to celebrate the sisterhood of women.

171

> *We need Heart Sisters to speak soft truth— even when the truth is hard.*

1. Heart Sisters can become Narrow Path friends. In chapter 3, we discussed the merits of Narrow Path friends. Narrow Path friends hold each other accountable to a Christian lifestyle through grace and love. There is no condemnation or judgment in a Narrow Path friendship—just ears to listen, a mouth to pray, and arms to hug. It's true there are times in which we must speak candid truth to our Narrow Path friends, but this would be for their benefit and not our own. Narrow Path friendships are about as real as they come.

In my own Narrow Path friendship, we once met consistently each week for lunch. It was our time to share prayer requests and an opportunity for an "iron to sharpen iron." Since we have eight children between the two of us, our weekly meetings have become a breakfast or lunch here and there and regular check-ins via phone or text. In the season of life of young children, talking on the phone can be a challenge, so texting an encouraging Bible verse, prayer, or even just a simple "Thinking of you today!" can mean so much.

2. Heart Sisters provide wise counsel. C. S. Lewis once said, "The next best thing to being wise oneself is to live in a circle of those who are." Isn't this so true? I have had moments when I suspect my plan of action is a little off, and I need to check myself before I wreck myself. While I think it's possible for an unbelieving friend to offer wisdom, I prefer to seek friends who are believers when I need advice because I know their advice will be biblically based. We need Heart Sisters to speak soft truth—even when the truth is hard.

3. **Heart Sisters help one another grow.** An iron sharpens iron. It's important to surround ourselves with friends who won't always be yes people or simply just tell us what we want to hear. We also don't want to have friends who would rather retreat from the relationship than have to confront us with stuff that's just plain hard. When we have a friend who will be lovingly candid with us, we are given an opportunity to listen and grow from our experience. Included in the long list of random how-to-do-life wisdom found in Proverbs is one of my favorite verses: "Listen to advice and accept discipline, and at the end you will be counted among the wise" (Proverbs 19:20). Being disciplined and instructed doesn't stop when our childhood is over. If you are wise, you allow it to continue through your entire life. As I tell my children, I can suggest they not do something, but the best lessons they will ever learn is through their own mistakes. Hopefully, they will have a friend who stands with them and candidly helps them learn the lesson.

4. **A Heart Sister stays by our side in times of adversity.** Tough stuff is going to happen. Author Glennon Melton once said, "Teach on, warriors. You are the first responders, the front line, the disconnection detectives and the best and only hope we have for a better world."[1] I love the idea of being a first responder, don't you? I certainly want to live my life as a first responder, much like my friend Jennifer.

Jennifer experienced the dreadful ups and downs of high school with me. She then walked through the painful end of my first marriage and a tumultuous period of dating that followed a few years later. I spoke at her mother's funeral; she was there when my father died. She shared my excitement when I met the real Mr. Right, and I asked her to be the only member of my

Humility gives us the ability to live happily.

wedding party when I married him. She sat next to me while I soaked my naked, hormonal body in the tub and cried that I should have never been trusted to bring a baby home from the hospital. Now *she's* a friend who's walked through adversity with me.

"A friend loves at all times and a [*sister*] is born for a time of adversity" (Proverbs 17:17). Yet while it's true we need to stand by our friends, it doesn't mean all boundaries are off. Sometimes people have made bad choices, and they want a coconspirator instead of a Heart Sister. Above all else, guard your heart.

5. A Heart Sister will work through a conflict with humility. You had to have known I was going to sneak in one more nugget about the virtues of humility, didn't you? When we find ourselves in the mess of a conflict with a friend, how we walk through said conflict is crucial. If we refuse to see our friend's perspective, deny responsibility, get defensive, and start to point out her faults, then we aren't handling the conflict with humility and the friendship will very likely end. As we've discussed before, it's not necessarily the mistakes we make that ruin a relationship—it's what we do afterwards that's most important. If a friend comes to you and wants to talk through something hard, it's your responsibility as a Heart Sister to listen to her perspective without interrupting. Apologize for hurting her in any way and take responsibility for what you need to own—then she will know you are a safe and authentic Heart Sister. Humility gives us the ability to live happily.

6. A Heart Sister forgives and allows for human weakness. We will mess up at times in our friendships with other women.

There will be moments when we say something we shouldn't have said. We might not handle a conflict with humility. Perhaps we've disappointed a friend. All of this happens because we are disabled by the flesh and we live in relationship with others. A Heart Sister understands she needs to give grace because there will be a time when she needs to receive grace.

7. **A Heart Sister loves your children almost as much as you do.** A really unexpected surprise happened with my own Heart Sisters: they love my children fiercely. Just the other day, one of my Heart Sisters was reading about a situation I wrote about on my blog in which my daughter was being bullied by another child. She called immediately, and when I picked up the phone, she said she was ready to pounce on that bully. I guess the Mama Bear instinct isn't limited to just our own children! The funny thing is, I feel exactly the same way about her children. Mess with any child in this Heart Sister posse, and you will have an army of tough mamas breathing down your neck! I'm certain there are few who are tougher than a group of mothers whose children have been hurt.

Because I don't have my own biological sisters, it's an incredible blessing to see a Heart Sister grab one of my children for a hug. I love watching my daughter be excited to tell Rachel about something happening in her life. My boys love to spend time with Katrina and know she will love on them the same way I do. All of my children know they're safe with Laurie, and they love playing at her house. Shelly teaches the little girls fun stuff to do with their hair. My Heart Sisters have taught me it really does indeed take a village to raise my children.

8. **A Heart Sister is candid and not honest.** As we discussed in the previous chapter, a true friend is not honest—she's candid.

She will talk to you about stuff that's hard, not for her own benefit, but for yours. A Heart Sister is willing to discuss the delicate issues because she cares about you and is committed to encouraging your relationship with God. Like any relationship, the one we have with God will often ebb and flow, but our Heart Sisters are the ones to point us back to truth. Sometimes we have to hear things that are difficult to hear so we can get re-centered and restore our relationship with God. Candid conversations between friends can convict and resurrect.

9. A Heart Sister always points us back to what's real and true. There are times when I can fall into a pit and begin to hear voices that are not from God. *I'm never enough for anyone. I'm not a very good writer. I should be ashamed for yelling at my children like that.* My guess is you are no stranger to thoughts like these, either. I've had moments when I have found myself so far removed from the truth that I've literally needed a Heart Sister to point out how off base I really am. I can always count on Melinda to say, "That's just not right or true." And she's usually correct: my thinking isn't right or true. This is when having friends who possess wisdom of how God rolls comes in handy. For example, when marital difficulties arise, the world will often encourage you to take a stand against how you're being treated and leave your spouse. On the hand, a friend who is a believer would likely encourage you to hang in a bit longer before you make a rash decision that will have a big impact. She understands marriage can sometimes be hard, but if you flee when it gets tough, you might miss out on a deeper relationship with your significant other. Heart Sisters who point us back to truth can encourage us to endure the times when life is just plain hard.

10. A Heart Sister recognizes the importance of marriage and encourages you to grow as a wife. She respects your family and understands they are your first commitment. Yes, marriage can be difficult. Yes, we can get angry with our partners and say things we probably shouldn't to our friends. But here's the thing: have you ever noticed how it's all right for you to say words against someone you love, but when others join in, you feel the need to defend the very person you were just putting down? While we may be angry with our husbands, we still love them and certainly don't need our friends pointing out their faults. We all have personality characteristics that make us human. None of us is easy to live with *all* of the time, right? When we start to go down the road of bemoaning our spouses, a Heart Sister will listen and offer advice (if you ask her) but will never put your spouse down or encourage you to leave—unless abuse is involved.

Similarly, a Heart Sister understands your family is your top priority. If you are having a rough night in which your children are cranky and your husband is not his best self, she won't pout because you had to cancel your plans with her. Life happens— let's give each other grace and move on.

11. A Heart Sister laughs with you. While there are definitely moments when we need to be serious, let's not ever discount the importance of fun! Laughter is a stress reliever, and my Heart Sisters are the ones who really understand a lot of the funny stuff that happens in my life—and I get the funny stuff that happens in theirs. Regular nights out with the girls are great, but if that's not possible for you in your season of life, be sure to pick up the phone and connect or Skype or whatever you need to do to get a good giggle. People who laugh more stress less.

12. A Heart Sister will do something for you without expecting anything in return. I once had a friend who kept score of her good deeds in our friendship. "I'll watch your kids for you if you will do this for me," she would offer. I was often frustrated with this because I believe that we do things for our friends because they're our friends. Of course, we don't want to become a doormat and take on, more than we should be expected to take on but I certainly don't have a "favor tally" on my refrigerator! I offer to help my friends because I love them and I want to help them—not because I expect to get something out of it, too.

On the other hand, if you feel as though a friend is taking advantage of your thoughtful heart, then it might be time to say no—but a true Heart Sister wouldn't put you in that position. There is an unspoken mutual respect between Heart Sisters, and it's a rare occasion when one takes advantage of another.

13. A Heart Sister is a prayer warrior who's on your side of the battle. Prayer works. They may not always be answered in the way we want them to be answered, but even in those disappointments, God is responding—He's just better at seeing the bigger picture than we are. Heart Sisters will pray for you as soon as you call in the troops and will continue praying until the issue is resolved. They will defend you if they hear anyone speaking not so greatly about you and will denounce the tactics of the enemy in the name of Jesus. There's nothing more beautiful than a friend willing to stop everything and pray on your behalf.

Ecclesiastes 4:9-10 tells us that "two are better than one, because they have a good return for their labor; if either of them falls down, one can help the other up. But pity anyone who falls and has no one to help him up!" Two people in prayer have a better return, and when two or more are gathered in His name, He is there (Matthew 18:20).

A Heart Sister is real with you. She cheers you on. She isn't afraid to say, "You're not alone. Me, too." She takes your children for an afternoon when you're at your wits' end and just need a break. She listens when your heart is broken, and she rejoices with you when it's not. She loves you without jealousy, comparison, and bitterness. She gives grace and needs grace and loves you for who you are right here, right now at this moment. She's your Heart Sister, and she adds a spice to your life that just makes it all taste better.

DISCUSSION QUESTIONS

1. *What qualities do you admire the most in a friend?*

2. *Do you have a covenant friendship? Is there someone you know who might be a good covenant friend? If so, pray it over and if you feel led, talk to her about the possibility of meeting regularly (or even just checking in by phone) to share prayer concerns and encouragement.*

3. *Have you ever had a friend betray a confidence? How did you feel? What did the experience teach you?*

4. *How can our friends encourage us in our marriages?*

5. *Have you ever advised a friend to do something you now regret? What did you learn from this?*

AFTERWORD

I'm so grateful you have chosen to learn more about friendship and how to be a Heart Sister. I hope you are now feeling inspired and committed to changing the culture of women from one of competition, backbiting, and envy to one of love, support, and encouragement. We need women like you who understand how to navigate healthy relationships with other women to make lasting, kingdom-impact change.

It is time for us to rise up, sister. We are better than how we are portrayed in *The Real Housewives of Beverly Hills*. We are better than the temptation of gossip. We are better than the envy that threatens to eat us alive. We are better than so much of the stuff that is a result of our flesh disability.

There are many stories throughout the Bible where you can see how much Jesus revered women. He loved Martha and Mary. Mary Magdalene. His mother, Mary. (All kinds of Marys.) The woman who touched His cloak. The woman at the well. The adulteress. Jesus cherished women and recognized their gifts.

It's time to be the change 88 percent of women want to see. It is time to reach out and love. Encourage. Help silence the voices telling her lies. Be there.

However, if you are feeling a little overwhelmed or hopeless, take heart. Don't give discouragement the final word because this will keep you locked in fear and very lonely. Simply start small. Pick up the phone and arrange a playdate with the mom you've been wanting to get to know. Join a MOPS group or a Bible study or ask a coworker to lunch. Most of all, pray that God will place healthy women in your life to be your Heart Sisters. Trust me—it's worth the courage it takes to put yourself out there.

I would love to hear your thoughts and stories. You can e-mail me at ncsnapp@gmail.com.

Thank you again for choosing to read *Heart Sisters*.

In Him,

Natalie

ACKNOWLEDGMENTS

When I began to entertain the thought of writing a book, many authors compared it to birthing a child. Like having a baby, birthing a book requires teams: a team to help write, a team to help edit, a team to help with marketing, and of course, a team that prays and talks you off the ledge when you're certain you didn't hear God's call correctly. *Heart Sisters* is no exception—quite a team has escorted her into the world.

First and foremost, "thank you" just doesn't seem like enough for Pamela Clements. Thank you, Pamela, for believing in the message of *Heart Sisters* and for taking a chance on a new author. This book would not exist without you. You have no idea how incredibly grateful I am for you, friend.

Jason, your quiet encouragements have kept me going when I wanted to throw in the towel. Thank you for being the master of "we'll make it work" and for knowing when I need to go to my room for a nap. There is no one—no one—I would rather walk through this life with than you.

Sarah, Samuel, and Spencer—thank you for understanding when Mommy needed to write. I knew you all understood what was happening when Spencer told his preschool teacher,

"Mom's out writing a book today." I hope you each know I would lay down writing and speaking for you in a heartbeat.

To my mother, Sarah Quick, and my Meemo, Mariam Lenox—thank you for the generational modeling of the importance of female friendships. Daughters learn from their mothers and grandmothers—I learned from the best.

Blythe Daniel, agent extraordinaire—thank you for being on my team, for offering your wise perspective, and for believing in *Heart Sisters*. I count you as one of God's richest blessings during this whole process.

To Lysa TerKeurst, Lindsay Stafford, Laurie Gattis, Karen Christian, Kenisha Bethea, Sheila Mangum, and Christina Clark—thank you for reading *Heart Sisters* and offering your encouragement, insights, and time. This book is better because of you all.

Karen Ehman, marketing guru and think-out-of-the-box lady—I cannot thank you enough for generously sharing what you've learned as an author over the years. You're amazing.

To all of the great people who worked on *Heart Sisters* from Abingdon Press—Pamela Clements, Lil Copan, Ramona Richards, Cat Hoort, and Brenda Smotherman—you took *Heart Sisters* to the next level. Thank you so much.

Jennifer, Katherine, Rachel J., Jen, Katrina, Rachel S., Laurie, Shelly, Melinda, Jill, Kelli, and Dana—thank you for teaching me how healthy female friendships are supposed to be and showing me how wonderful they truly are. You all are the redemption of many past hurts.

And I save the best for last—thank you to Jesus. You took a girl who was a hot mess of despair, confusion, and anger and pulled her out of a deep pit fifteen years ago. I am proof that You will use anyone—*anyone*—to deliver Your message. May these words honor You. I will follow You forever. Literally.

NOTES

1. But Do We Really *Need* Girlfriends?

1. University of California Los Angeles, "UCLA Researchers Identify Key Biobehavioral Pattern Used by Women to Manage Stress," *Science Daily*. www.sciencedaily.com/releases /2000/05/000522082151.htm (accessed December 15, 2014).

2. Shelley E. Taylor, *The Tending Instinct* (New York: Henry Holt, 2002), 21.

3. Gale Berkowitz, "UCLA Study of Friendship Among Women," www.scribd.com/doc/16043143/Ucla-Study-on-Friendship-Among -Women.

4. John Mariani, "Shaking Up the Salt Myth: This Thanksgiving, Go Ahead and Pour on the Sodium Chloride," *New York Daily News* (November 24, 2011). www.nydailynews.com/opinion /shaking-salt-myth-thanksgiving-pour-sodium-chloride-article -1.982027.

5. SaltWorks, "Salt Uses and Tips," www.saltworks.us/salt_info /salt-uses-and-tips.asp.

3. Seek and You Will Find

1. Kim Culbertson, *The Liberation of Max McTrue* (Amazon Digital: Bookbaby, 2012).

5. The Forgiveness Business

1. Rebecca Nichols Alonzo, *The Devil in Pew Number Seven* (Carol Stream, IL: Tyndale, 2010), 248.

6. Blurred Lines: Establishing Holy Boundaries

1. Marianne Williamson, *A Return to Love: Reflections on the Principles of "A Course in Miracles"* (New York: HarperCollins, 1992), 190.
2. Donald J. Davidson, ed., *The Wisdom of Theodore Roosevelt* (New York: Citadel, 2003), 48.
3. Graham Cooke, "Grace Growers," *Lutheran Renewal* 236 (October 2006): 1–2.

7. Texting, Twitter, and Tumblr: Friendship Etiquette in a Digital World

1. Kit Murray, "Do We Need to Untangle?" *The Advocate* (November 4, 2014). http://msumadvocate.com/2014/11/04/do-we-need-to-untangle/.
2. Jennifer Soong, "When Technology Addiction Takes Over Your Life," www.webmd.com/mental-health/addiction/features/when-technology-addiction-takes-over-your-life?page=3+-+Technology+addiction%2C+why+we+need+rest%2C+how+to+work+smart.

8. Tomorrow's Heart Sisters: Teaching Our Daughters to Be Good Friends

1. Kayla Webley, "Why Women Are Their Own Worst Enemy," *Time* (November 14, 2010), http://content.time.com/time/nation/article/0,8599,2031310,00.html.
2. Dannah Gresh, *8 Great Dates for Moms and Daughters* (Eugene, OR: Harvest House, 2010).
3. More information about The Whatever Girls can be found at www.thewhatevergirls.com.
4. Meredith, "Who Is She?" www.gammawomen.com/html/who.html.

10. What Does a Heart Sister Not Do?

1. Graham Cooke, "Overcoming Negativity Through Rest: Our Language Is Evidence of Our Position," audio podcast, July 16, 2013.
2. Tim Kimmel, *Grace-Based Parenting* (Nashville: Thomas Nelson, 2005).

11. What Does a Heart Sister Do?

1. Glennon Doyle Melton, "Share This With All the Schools, Please" Momastery blog post, January 30, 2014, http://momastery.com/blog/2014/01/30/share-schools/.

ABOUT THE AUTHOR

Natalie Chambers Snapp is first and foremost a follower of Jesus, then wife to Jason, and mom to one spunky daughter and two spirited sons. Choosing to follow Jesus at twenty-seven, Natalie became passionate about sharing the grace, mercy, and truth of God's love regardless of one's track record. She lives in Indiana with her crew where she writes about faith in the everyday mundane.

Natalie is a regular contributor to The M.O.B. Society, Deeper Waters, and the Whatever Girls Ministry. Her work has also been featured at (in)courage and in *Life: Beautiful* magazine. The outpourings of her heart can be found at www .nataliesnapp.com in the fleeting moments between being a wife and mother and folding piles of laundry that never go away.